ARLECDON

A JOURNEY THROUGH TIME

By
Arlecdon History Group

Published by Arlecdon History Group

2008

ISBN 978-0-9544112-2-0

Printed and bound by the Firpress Group Ltd. Workington

Arlecdon History Project

Following the exhibition and production of the booklet, *'Arlecdon's Acre'* in 2005, as part of the activities to celebrate the centenary of the re-furbishment of St Michael's Church, the Arlecdon History Group decided to continue to collect stories and photographs about the area.

Their aim was, not to produce a definitive history, which had already been well documented in the Rev. E.H. Sugden's *'History of Arlecdon and Frizington'* in 1897 (updated by Richard Byers in 1907), but to record incidents in the lives of residents, focusing on the 20th century, a period of great change.

The group members have been encouraged and supported by the management and staff of Frizington Community Development Centre and Library and by a generous grant from the Lottery Heritage Fund. This has financed the production of this book and the accompanying DVD, *'A Stroll Around Arlecdon, Past and Present'*. The recording of the memorial inscriptions in the churchyard has also been completed.

We hope our efforts will stir a few memories for the present inhabitants and the many who now reside further afield, but whose hearts remain in *'Arlecdon's Acre'*.

Acknowledgments and thanks

We are most grateful for the generosity of local people and the many in other areas of the country, who have allowed us to share their memories and have loaned us treasured documents and photographs.

Also our thanks go to:-

The Members of Arlecdon Age Concern Lunch Club

Children and Staff of Arlecdon Primary School

St Michael's Church Council

Staff at Whitehaven Record Office

Staff at the Beacon, Whitehaven

Staff at Firpress Printers Ltd

Cumbrian Railways Association

Contents

Arlecdon and District

Arlecdon is a small village situated about six miles north east of Whitehaven. It forms part of the parish of Arlecdon and Frizington, which also includes Asby, Rowrah and Winder. Eskett is in the parish of Lamplugh but because of its proximity and connections with Arlecdon it has been included.

Until the 19th century the main occupation was farming. The discovery of coal, iron ore, lime and freestone (sandstone) and the coming of the railway meant an increase in population which necessitated more houses being built. Nearby quarries provided some building material.

The original village was the nucleus for a larger one, spreading over the hill, and along Arlecdon Parks Road. The two Inns were, 'The Sun', where once church records were kept and 'The Hound' on the main road. The Liberal Reading Room, built in1891, contained 200 volumes. Mona Street, from where one can see the Isle of Man, may derive its name from Julius Caesar's calling the Isle of Man 'Mona'. The Vicarage has had various sites, and now stands on the road to Frizington. The Post Office also moved around, but by 1931 was situated at 51 Arlecdon Road, with a shop next door where the General Store and Post Office is today.

By 1813 Arlecdon had race meetings on Common Side, (Murton Park). Arlecdon Moor was the venue for wrestling matches. Cattle fairs were held in April, June, and September on the Fair Field now the playing field.

The population rose from 400 in 1801 to 6,500 in 1881, but by 1991 had declined to 3,500*.

In the 18th century children were taught by the clergy. In 1725 the Rev. Baxter taught children in St. Michael's Church Chancel. Later there was a school near Arlecdon House. In the 1820s there was a small school behind 23 Arlecdon Road. In 1860 there were 35 pupils. It was known as the Arlecdon Parochial School. A Sunday School, (now a private dwelling) and Arlecdon Board School were built in 1878. This school was developed to accommodate 300 children aged 5 to 14 years. There were originally 54 pupils but due to influx of families as the mines opened, the numbers rapidly grew. It was extended in 1889 and 1899 to house 400 children. One of the headmasters in the early 20th Century was a local man, William Branthwaite who was born in Lamplugh. Elizabeth Dixon, born in Arlecdon, was taught there and became a pupil teacher. There are approximately 50 children in the school today.

In the late 19th and early 20th centuries the industries were farming, coal and iron ore mining, limestone and freestone quarrying and a tile works. Although the coal mines, (Asby, Moorside, Dean Moor and Oatlands), employed 218 underground and 95 surface workers in the years between 1908 and 1933 they are all now abandoned. Iron ore followed suit. Farming continues today but mechanisation has reduced the numbers of farm workers required. A large number of the residents work at Sellafield which is the major employer for this area.

The 2001 census recorded a population of 3,675 in the Parish of Arlecdon and Frizington.

The Church and Churchyard

The Rev. E H Sugden in his book *'The History of Arlecdon and Frizington'*, believed that the site of Arlecdon church was a very ancient one. He pointed out that although the church was inconveniently situated, being some distance from the village, it had at one time stood near a substantial dwelling known as Moorside Hall.

The restoration of the church one hundred years ago uncovered evidence of previous structures. The discovery of a 13th century grave slab during the 1903-05 alterations, together with the 12th century chancel arch, appears to confirm its early origins.

The refurbishment of the church and the building of the tower a century ago were only made possible by the generosity of Mrs Elizabeth Higgins, wife of a former curate and daughter of the Fletcher family of High House, Parkside.

A database of memorial inscriptions provides a useful resource for family historians and is particularly important where the stones are susceptible to wear and damage. A recording of the inscriptions in Arlecdon churchyard has been completed and will be available through the church, the Whitehaven Record Office and the Cumbria Family History Society.

1900 to 1909

Joseph Green

Builder of Arlecdon Church Tower 1905

Joseph Green of Pardshaw Lee-Gate, whose firm undertook the restoration of Arlecdon Church in 1905, came from a long line of builders. The firm was founded by his grandfather who was a dry-stone waller and built barns and farm buildings.

Joseph's father, John, expanded the business substantially from the 1860s but it was Joseph who developed the skills required to build churches, which included Kirkland Mission Church, Rowrah Chapel and the church at Great Clifton.

Almost all the male family members were trained in carpentry or became stone-masons and contributed to the business. In 1881 there were 34 men and 3 boys working for the firm.

Joseph Green died on 21st September 1907 aged 71 years and his obituary in the Cumberland Paquet describes him as having an immense capacity for work, jealously guarding the honour of his name by often destroying what he considered not satisfactorily built.

His funeral took place at Dean and among those present were; Mr T Dixon of Rheda, Mr A J S Dixon of Lorton Hall, Mr J H Jefferson of Hundith Hill, Mr J M Dickinson of Hames Hall,

Mr Green on the church tower

Captain Mirehouse, Loweswater, Mr J Watson of South Mosses, Mr J Brown and Mr J Wood of Lamplugh, Mr R Salked of Ullock Mains, Mr David Dickinson of Kidburngill and many more including his workmen and neighbours.

After the death of Joseph, the business was carried on by his nephew Herbert Green until the outbreak of the First World War when Herbert enlisted in the Scots Guards and was awarded a Certificate of Gallantry in September 1915. He was later awarded the Military Medal and accepted a commission as Second Lieutenant before being killed by a sniper in October 1917 at the third Battle of Ypres. By sheer coincidence Ted Blacklock, later to become manager of Rowrah Co-op, served in the war alongside Herbert's brother Alf and wrote home about Herbert's promotion.

Various members of the Green family carried on the building trade including Henry who built houses at Distington and Edwin, a Frizington joiner, the grandfather of Mr John Craig of Sevenoaks, Kent, who kindly supplied the information and photographs for this section.

Not everyone agreed with the changes to what had been a humble country church.

This poem by Mrs Mulcaster, formerly Miss Dickinson of Kidburngill illustrates her feelings.

Arlecdon Church – 1906

Can this be really Arlecdon
This structure tall and proud?
A stranger passing, scarce would know
Tis so changed on every hand.
Yet still it's on the self same spot
My forefathers used to know
But builder's hands have been at work
And there's little now to show
Except arch and windows still are left
Left of the years long past
When things were humbler plainer far
But a change has come at last
But give to me the dear old church
That's still by the lone highway
T'were more in keeping with the place
Than the one that's there today.

Mrs Mary Mulcaster
Napier House, Workington
October 1926

Arlecdon church prior to 1905 restoration

Consecration Service 1905

Church today with War Memorial

1910 to 1919

The Great War 1914 - 1918

During the First World War, 1914 – 1918, about 90 youths and men from Arlecdon Parish enlisted into the Forces. By 1918, 23 men had been killed or died from their injuries. Some of the men were buried in St Michael's Churchyard, Arlecdon, but some never returned home and were buried in various cemeteries in France and other localities.

In 1917 the Parish published a 'Roll of Honour with Colours' which was sent out to the brave men in the battle fields. Many of these men were awarded medals and distinctions for their bravery.

Our research has provided us with some interesting details, photographs, and stories of some of the servicemen who were killed and also of those who thankfully survived the Great War.

PRIVATE JOSEPH EDWARD DIXON

Private Joseph Edward Dixon (Joe), son of Edward and Sarah Elizabeth of Eskett Farm, Winder, joined 2/8 Battalion Lancashire Fusiliers as a volunteer. During the first World War, Joe was in action near Vimy Ridge. He sent a letter to his sister Marion on 25th April 1917.

Dear Marion

Just a few lines to say that I am quite well, hoping you are the same. I received the parcel alright, it was a bit broke but not much. Do not send any more eggs as they got smashed! I am sorry to hear that ……. was wounded and had to go back to the trenches again. Joe Stainton is wounded also Harold Mandle from Cleator Moor, Joe Stainton was wounded in No Man's Land and we had a job to fetch him out on account of the shell holes and barbed wire. I helped to carry him in. Mandle was buried by a shell and has hurt his legs, otherwise alright. Joe was wounded in three places but not seriously but bad enough, I hope so to carry him to England.

What do you think of the war now and the good work they are doing on Vimy Ridge. We are not so far from there. I am sending you the ROLL OF HONOUR. Now I will close with love to you all and hoping the war will soon be over. Joe

A few weeks later on 15th May 1917 Joe was killed aged 19 years. His name is commemorated on the 'Loos Memorial' in France. *The letter and information by kind permission of the Dixon family.*

PARISH of ARLECDON

ROLL OF HONOUR
1914 - 1918.

✳ **"Their Name Liveth For Evermore."** ✳

ATKINSON, GEORGE *16th September, 1916*
BLACKBURN, WALTER *3rd April, 1917*
BLAND, ALBERT WILSON *17th December, 1916*
BRIGGS, WILLIAM *21st March, 1918*
BROWN, JOHN *24th May, 1915*
BULMAN, CHRISTOPHER *15th May, 1916*
CASSON, ROBERT *16th May, 1915*
DIXON, JAMES *1st March, 1917*
DIXON, JOSEPH EDWARD *15th May, 1917*
FISHER, JAMES *31st August, 1916*
HODGSON, ALBERT *22nd July, 1917*

JOHNSTON, ISAAC *23rd April, 1917*
JOHNSTON, JOHN *23rd April, 1917*
LITTLE, JOHN ROBERT *28th December, 1915*
LITTLE, WILLIAM JAMES *19th October, 1916*
MAHONY, CORNELIUS *25th September, 1915*
METCALFE, JOSEPH ANTHONY *20th Aug., 1917*
PASCOE, JAMES *11th December, 1918*
PRITT, WILLIAM HEAD *1st April, 1918*
ROUTLEDGE, JOHN *26th February, 1916*
STAINTON, WILLIAM *7th February, 1916*
WILLIAMSON, JOHN JOSEPH *14th March, 1917*

WILSON, JAMES STANLEY *24th October, 1918*

ADAMS, JAMES
ADAMS, STANLEY
ATKINSON, JACKSON
ATKINSON, ROBERT
ATKINSON, WILLIAM
BELL, JAMES, M.M.
BELL, JOSEPH
BIRNEY, JONATHAN JAMES
BOAK, ISAAC
BRAGG, JOHN
BRAGG, ROBERT HENRY
BRANTHWAITE, ERIC WILLIAM
BRANTHWAITE, JOHN THOMAS
BRIGGS, JAMES
BRIGGS, JOHN
BRIGGS, MATTHEW THOMPSON
CASSON, ALEXANDER
CASSON, JOSEPH
CLEMENTS, ABRAHAM
CLEMENTS, JOHN
CLEMENTS, JOSEPH
COULTHARD, JOHN HENRY
DAVIDSON, JAMES
DICKINSON, DANIEL
DICKINSON, JOHN
DIXON, EVAN
DIXON, JOSEPH
DIXON, NEWTON
DOVER, JOHN HODGSON
DRAKEFORD, JOHN CHARLES
DUNNACHIE, JAMES RICHMOND
FISHER, ALBERT
FITZWILLIAMS, RICHARD
FLETCHER, HODGSON PARKER
FLETCHER, JOHN, D.C.M.
FLETCHER, JOSEPH WHINN
FORRESTER, JOSEPH
FORRESTER, ROBERT WILLIAM
FOSTER, JOHN
FREARS, JAMES WILLIAM
GATE, ISAAC DICKINSON
GIBSON, DAVID
GIBSON, HARRY

GIBSON, JAMES
GIBSON, JAMES FEARON
GIBSON, JAMES FISHWICK EDWARDS
GILMORE, JOHN COLVIN
GOGGINS, JOSEPH
GRAHAM, JOHN
GRAHAM, JOHN ROBERT
HELLON, JOHN RICHARD
HELLON, MATTHEW
HIND, GEORGE
HIND, JOSEPH
HODGSON, JOSEPH HARRISON
IRVING, FRANCIS JOHN
IRVING, JOHN RICHARD
IRVING, WILLIAM HAROLD
JACKSON, THOMAS
JACKSON, THOMAS
JAMES, THOMAS
JOHNSTON, NICHOLAS
KEY, ISAAC
KEY, WILLIAM
KIRKBRIDE, THOMAS WILLIAM
KNEEN, HENRY EDWIN
LAWSON, ARTHUR
LETTIMER, JOHN JAMES
LITTLE, JARED
MASON, JOSEPH ROUTLEDGE
MASON, SIDNEY
MATTINSON, ALBERT LAWRENCE
McALEESE, JOHN
McCREADIE, GEORGE
McCREADIE, JOHN
McCREADIE, LAWSON ARMSTRONG
MERRITT, WILLIAM JOHN
MURRAY, HARRISON, M.M.
MURRAY, WILLIAM
NICHOLSON, ANTHONY BLACKSTOCK
NICHOLSON, EDWARD
PARKER, WILLIAM
RAY, ADAM NIXON
RAY, DOUGLAS HODGSON

RAY, JOHN ERNEST
REAY, JOHN McKNIGHT
REID, JOHN
RICHARDSON, DANIEL
ROBINSON, GEORGE BARNES
ROBINSON, HENRY
ROBINSON, JOHN
ROBINSON, JOHN, M.M.
ROBINSON, WILLIAM, D.C.M.
WILSON, D.C.M.
RODGERS, DANIEL
SANDERSON, GEORGE
SAVAGE, ROBERT
SAVILLE, WILLIAM
SESSFORD, JOHN JOSEPH
SEWELL, JOHN BRISCOE
SHAW, TOM HARRISON
SHERWEN, PETER
SHERWEN, SAMUEL
SHERWEN, WILLIAM
SISSON, AARON
SISSON, GEORGE
SISSON, THOMAS
SLACK, THOMAS
SLATER, SYDNEY ALBERT
SMITHSON, JOHN
STAINTON, ALEXANDER
STAINTON, JAMES
STAINTON, THOMAS, M.M.
TOMLINSON, WILLIAM
TYSON, MOSES HUDDLESTON
TYSON, JAMES
WALTON, THOMAS HENRY
WATSON, MARTIN, M.M.
WEIGHMAN, GEORGE
WEIGHMAN, JOSEPH
WHITTEN, THOMAS
WIGHAM, JOSEPH
WILSON, JONATHAN
WILSON, ROBINSON
WOOD, WILLIAM
WOOSNAM, WILLIAM

✳ **"They were a wall unto us both by night and by day."** ✳

ARLECDON WAR MEMORIAL

1914—1918
IN PROUD AND LOVING
MEMORY OF

ATKINSON, GEORGE 16 SEPTEMBER 1916
BLACKBURN, WALTER 3 APRIL 1917
BLAND, ALBERT WILSON 17 DECEMBER 1916
BRIGGS, WILLIAM 21 MARCH 1918
BROWN, JOHN 24 MAY 1915
BULMAN, CHRISTOPHER 15 MAY 1916
CASSON, ROBERT 16 MAY 1915
DIXON, JAMES 1 MARCH 1917
DIXON, JOS. EDWARD 15 MAY 1917
FISHER, JAMES 31 AUGUST 1916
HODGSON, ALBERT 22 JULY 1917
JOHNSTON, ISAAC 23 APRIL 1917
JOHNSTON, JOHN 23 APRIL 1917
LITTLE, JOHN ROBERT 28 DECEMBER 1915
LITTLE, Wm. JAMES 19 OCTOBER 1916
MAHONEY, CORNELIUS 25 SEPTEMBER 1915
METCALFE, JOSEPH ANTHONY 20 AUGUST 1917
PASCOE, JAMES 11 DEC 1918
PRITT, Wm. HEAD 1 APRIL 1918
ROUTLEDGE, JOHN 26 FEB 1916
STAINTON, WILLIAM 7 FEB 1916
WILLIAMSON, Jnr. Jos. 14 MARCH 1917
WILSON, JAMES STANLEY 24 OCTOBER 1918

THEIR NAME LIVETH FOR EVERMORE

1939— 1945

WILLIAM BRIGGS 14 JUNE 1944
DONALD BROWN 2 JULY 1942
JOHN YOUNG CHARLTON 2 DEC 1944
WILLIAM TYSON GILL 30 MARCH 1943
JOHN WATSON LEATHES 1 NOV 1944

WILFRED RAY 1944
ROBINSON STABLES 22 DEC 1942
ANTHONY FERGUSON 20 JUNE 1967

James Dixon

Walter Blackburn

JAMES DIXON

James, son of William and Jane Dixon of Low Arlecdon was born in 1887. He married Martha Fisher on 24th May 1899. James emigrated to Canada circa 1907 to work as a coal miner. He joined the regular Canadian Infantry and served in the 1st World War in France. James was killed in action on 1st March 1917 on Vimy Ridge in France and was given a soldier's grave on the battlefield.

Information and photo contributed by Jean Birdsall

WALTER BLACKBURN

Walter, son of Joshua and Eleanor Blackburn of Parks Road, Arlecdon was born in 1890. Walter emigrated to New Zealand. During the 1st World War Walter joined the Canterbury Regiment NZEF and served in France. He was killed on 3rd April 1917 and buried in Bailleul Communal Cemetery Extension (NORD).

Information contributed by Nan Wilson

JAMES ADAMS

James Adams (Jim), son of Thomas and Mary Adams of Arlecdon was born 1897 the youngest of 13 children. His father was killed in Parkside Mine, Winder several months before Jim's birth. Jim enlisted in the Border Regiment on 7th January 1915 aged 18 years and served in the 1st World War in France. He was injured several times and spent time in hospital in Malta, being discharged from service 12th November 1918. On returning to Arlecdon, Jim suffered ill health and attacks of Malaria but resumed work in the Iron Ore mines. Jim died in 1958 leaving a wife Janie and a daughter Frances.

Information and photo: - Janie Adams and daughter, Frances Rudd.

STANLEY ADAMS

Stanley Adams who was James's older brother also served in the 1st World War and returned, but continued to make his career in the army.

DOUGLAS HODGSON RAY

Extract from St Michael's Parish Church, Arlecdon, Magazine 4th May 1916

> *'It is with much regret that I record here that Douglas Ray has been some what severely wounded in the head and is lying at one of the hospitals in Boulogne. Fortunately he is conscious and the most recent news gives hope. At the services on Sunday last, our Roll of Honour day, Douglas was much in our thoughts and prayers. Mr & Mrs Ray went to France yesterday to see their son, and our hope and prayer is that they may find him much better than anticipated.'*

JOHN ROUTLEDGE

Private John Routledge, aged 40 years, was the son of Thomas and Jane Routledge of Arlecdon and died on 26th February 1916. He served with the 'D' Company, 3rd Regiment, South African Infantry.

Whitehaven News 9th March 1916

Information from deceased's brother, Joseph, of Hodgson Court, Egremont

"John was in the Cumberland Militia for 6 years. He went to South Africa and was transferred to the Oxford Light Infantry and fought through the Boer War being given two medals each with a bar. One was inscribed 'South Africa 1901 and South Africa 1902'. The other was inscribed 'Orange Free State and Cape Colony'.

He visited his native land 5 years ago and then journeyed to S.A. and on the outbreak of war he joined Botha's Forces in German North West Africa. He fought in several engagements but came through without a scratch.

He then came to England with his contingent. After training in the south of England, they were ordered to Egypt in December last where, during an engagement on February 26th. he was wounded and died on the same day".

The Routledge family had lived in Arlecdon for many years. John's grandfather Joseph died at

John Routledge's headstone in Alexandria Military and War Memorial Cemetery (Chatby), Egypt

Tilekiln Cottage in 1892. He was a thorough sportsman and enjoyed a good day's hunting and fishing. He owned considerable property at Arlecdon, Frizington Road, and Rowrah. He was a large shareholder in the London and North Western and Furness Railway Companies.

In his will dated 1859 he left effects to the value of £1,921 -10s-2d to his son Thomas who was the father of Private John Routledge.

Information kindly contributed by Mr Denis Magean of Harrington

THE JOHNSTONE BROTHERS

Extract from St Michael's Parish Church Magazine, Arlecdon

'Isaac and John, sons of David and Mary Johnstone of Rowrah Road, sadly, were both killed on the same day, 23rd April 1917 whilst serving in France. Isaac aged 26 was married to Rose and served in the Argyll and Sutherland Highlanders 11th Battalion. He was buried in the Canadian Cemetery number 2 Neuville, St. Yaast, France.'

John, aged 23 served in the Border Regiment and is commemorated on the Arras Memorial, France.'

QUARTER MASTER SERGEANT JOHN FLETCHER, D.C.M.

Extract from St Michael's Parish Church Magazine, Arlecdon, 8th January 1917

'Our D.C.M – Company Quarter Master Sergeant John Fletcher D.C.M. – has arrived home on a few weeks leave. It has been in my mind ever since the great honour was conferred upon him, to arrange for him a public welcome at Arlecdon. The opportunity has now come. On discussing the matters with our workers the other evening it was decided to give this public welcome at the concert in connection with the Old Folks Reunion on Wednesday 17th January 1917 at 7.30pm. I am confident our people will come in crowds to acclaim this gallant young son of our village. Two of John's old friends, Robert Marshall and William James Middleton are making a little collection for him so that the function on the 17th will include a presentation as well. I am pleased to be able to announce that Captain Churchill-Longman as kindly agreed to make the presentation.'

PRIVATE TOM STAINTON

Extract from St Michael's Parish Church Magazine, Arlecdon, 4th February 1918

'Tom Stainton has been awarded the Military Medal for carrying in wounded on 3rd December and also on the 6th December 1918 under heavy fire from the enemy. Tom, who is in the Canterbury Infantry, New Zealand, is an Arlecdon lad. Seven years ago he emigrated to South Africa and after staying there 3½ years, he then went on to New Zealand. When he had been there six months, war broke out and he joined up, coming over with the first New Zealand contingent.

He was all through Dardavilly Expedition and was severely wounded in the chest. He also served in Egypt. He was drafted to France and had many narrow escapes from death and was twice buried. He was on leave from France last week and left Arlecdon on Tuesday to spend a couple of days with his sister who resides at Manchester, before going back to France.'

The Briggs Family Sacrifice

I first became aware of William Briggs on seeing his name carved into the white stone wall near to that of my great uncle William H Adams, in Bay 1 of the ARRAS Memorial, in the Faubourg-d'Amiens Cemetery, Pas-de-Calais, France. The memorial commemorates 35,000 British, South African & New Zealand servicemen who lost their lives on the battlefields around ARRAS, between the spring of 1916 and August 1918, and who have no known grave.

A section of the wall in Bay 1 is dedicated to the men of the Royal Field Artillery, the regiment in which Driver Willam Briggs and Gunner William Adams served. The two men were comrades in the 160th Wearside Brigade R.F.A., (although neither of them came from the Sunderland area), and both died of their wounds, received in the fighting around the village of Croisilles (8km south of Arras), on the 21st March 1918.

William Briggs was born in December 1889, near to Red Beck, Eskett, the eldest son and second child to Mr John Cowan Briggs, an Iron Ore Miner, originally from Cleator Moor and Mrs Isabella Briggs. The Briggs family moved around the area before settling down at 162 Frizington Road, Arlecdon at sometime around the turn of the last century.

The young William Briggs remained in the village of Arlecdon and followed his father into the local mines. In 1913, W B married Miss Jane Ann Whitten and the following year the couple celebrated the birth of their first child, a girl named Maggie. On the 22nd January 1915, a second child William (Jnr) arrived to complete the family.

William Briggs (Snr) was already member of the R.F.R.A. (As a Royal Artillery pre-war reservist) and at the outbreak of WW1 would have been amongst the first wave of non regular soldiers, to be mobilised and sent to France and the Western Front. Although it has not been possible to follow William's military service at the front, (unfortunately his army records were amongst those destroyed in the blitz of WW2), we do know, from other sources that he also served with the 3rd Divisional Ammunition Column, prior to joining the 106 Brigade R.F.A.

The good people of Arlecdon honoured the men of the village, who were serving in the armed forces, by commissioning a poster in 1917, entitled; 'Parish of Arlecdon Roll of Honour'.

Under the heading, 'With the Colours', can be clearly seen the names of William Briggs and his brother John Briggs who had joined the M.G.C (Machine Gun Corp).

The Great Battle of 21st March 1918 claimed more casualties than any other day in the history of the British Army. More than 39,000 men were lost. The German Army would also lose over 40,000 men on that day, and the offensive would ultimately decide the outcome of the conflict.

In the weeks after the Battle, over 29,000 letters were delivered to the next of kin of men reported missing or killed in action on the 21st March. One such message would have arrived in Arlecdon, at the home of Mrs Jane Briggs, informing the family that Driver 11970 Briggs was missing, believed to have died of his wounds.

Little is known of the suffering and anguish of the widowed Mrs Briggs. We can assume that alone with two small children to bring up and with little assistance from the government of the day that life was extremely hard.

The peace in Europe was relatively short lived and once more the call to arms was answered by the Briggs Family of Arlecdon. On the 30th May 1940, William Briggs (Jnr) joined up and was posted to serve with the 114 Battalion, the South Lancashire Regiment. After four years home service and training William (Jnr) embarked for France on the 14th June 1944, part of the post 'D Day' invasion force. Private 1964070 William Briggs (Jnr.) was killed in action that same day. He is buried at the La Delivrande War Cemetery, Douvres, France, less than 25 miles away from the place that his father William Briggs (Senior) had been killed 26 years earlier.

Once again the postal service would be charged with delivering a message, from War Office, to the home of Mrs J.A. Briggs, informing her of the news of the death of her only son.

Information researched and kindly contributed by Mr Philip Adams

P.S. A telegram delivery boy was often employed to deliver the sad news of a soldier's injury or death. On one such occasion, during the Second World War, no delivery boy was available and the Arlecdon Postmaster had to deliver the message himself. The addressee of the telegram lived at Winder and so the Postmaster had to travel there by bus. By coincidence, the recipient was a passenger on the same bus but the poor Postmaster had to follow her home and hand the envelope to her once she was inside the house as this was the Post Office ruling. It must have been the most uncomfortable bus journey he had ever made in his life!

Some more extracts from St Michael's Church Magazine

Arlecdon Vicarage – August 1915
Christmas Parcels for our Soldiers

'The members of the Girls Friendly Society with the help of others are working vigorously in the preparation of comforts for our soldiers. And the Sunday School Teachers are gathering from themselves and their scholars, chocolates, cigarettes, handkerchiefs and other acceptable things in order that together – the GFS and the SS – they may send a delightful Christmas parcel to each of the soldiers from this parish. It is a splendid work. Gifts of any kind will be gladly received by any SS Teacher, member of the GFS, Mrs Parker or myself. The sooner we have them the better, as we are anxious to send off the parcels as early as possible.

Mrs Irving, 7 Arlecdon Road, has handed me £1 13s, 6d., the proceeds of a drawing, to be spent on cigarettes for our soldiers; and Miss Jackson, Result, has sent 10/- towards the Christmas parcels. Socks, mittens, handkerchiefs, soaps, etc., have also been received. Many grateful thanks to all givers.'

H Hunter Parker

1st December 1917
Christmas Gifts for our Soldiers

'After very careful consideration and consultation with those interested, it has been decided to send our men this Christmas, 10/- each instead of a parcel. And this is largely for two reasons. Now that there are to be found, wherever there are soldiers, YMCA huts and Church Army huts, at which the men are for themselves able to procure just exactly what they may need, it seems a misuse of money to send parcels entailing so much use of calico, paper and postage. Also it has been found, when an occasional parcel has been returned, that the

sweet loaves had suffered very considerably and were unfortunately flavoured with the other contents of the parcel. I have confidence that the men will like the change. Anyhow, if they don't, we can at Easter, should the necessity still be laid upon us, revert to the old system. The gift of 10/- to each man is being sent with the good wishes of the whole parish for a joyous Christmas and a speedy and safe return to the dear old home.'

H Hunter Parker

4th November 1917

James Tyson

'James Tyson lost a leg fighting for his country. He has now been treated in this country and has been supplied with an artificial leg. At the present moment he is spending a furlough with his parents, Mr and Mrs William Tyson of Arlecdon Road. Although his leg was taken off above the knee you will, when next you meet him, have difficulty in discerning which is the artificial leg, so admirably does it bend at the knee and spring at the foot. It is a marvel of modern skill.'

H Hunter Parker

1st December 1917

Two More Distinctions

'It was with great delight that our parish received the news that two more of our men had gained distinctions. Harrison Murray and Martin Watson have each won the Military Medal. To win distinctions such as the Military Medal in such a war as this, implies very great bravery. Our hearty congratulations to these two brave young men and also to their parents.'

H Hunter Parker

1915

The Choir Boys – 1915

'When the war broke out, our choristers, bell ringers and the Sunday School teachers passed a resolution foregoing their usual summer trip so long as the war lasts. This was and is most commendable and has been most favourably commented on both in and out of the parish. Children, however, are but children, and our SS teachers although foregoing their own trip were unanimous in granting one to the SS children. To complete in a modest way this recognition of the young people, Mrs Parker gave the choir boys tea at the Anglers' Hotel on the 10ᵗʰ August. Miss and Mr Ives kindly walked with the boys by way of the fields and woods.'

H Hunter Parker

Choir boys circa 1915

Extracts from Whitehaven News 13th June 1918

'News has been received by Mrs Walton, Rowrah, from her husband, Private Thomas H. Walton, Border Regiment, that he is a prisoner of war in Germany.'

'Mr and Mrs Thomas Birney, Arlecdon, have also received a postcard from their son, Private Jonathan Birney, stating that he is wounded and a prisoner of war.'

Both are interned at Linberg.

'Private W Briggs, Arlecdon, is reported missing. Word has been received by his wife from France that he was wounded, but owing to the heavy attack made by the Germans, they were obliged to leave him. (Private Briggs actually died on 21st March 1918 – see account by P.W Adams)

'Word has also been received by Mr and Mrs Joseph Bell, Arlecdon, that their son, Private James Bell had been wounded in the head and arms in France. This is the second time that Private Bell has been wounded.'

Arlecdon Social Activities

Arlecdon seems to have been rich in Social Group activities. One such group was the St. Michael's Guild or Debating Society, which seems to have held meetings on a regular basis during the winter months. A wide range of subjects were debated, such as 'Land Reform', 'The Insurance Act', 'Froebels Principles on Education' , 'Compulsory Military Service', 'Should Trade Disputes be settled by arbitration?', 'How we learned to count', 'Whether England was deteriorating', even 'Whether a man was better or worse for having a glass of beer', among other diverse topics.

Field days were held, which started with a procession through the village accompanied by a Band and Morris Dancers. Children were given tea supplied by Mrs. Higgins. Children's sports followed, also adult sports and a social in the Church Rooms also took place.

Another Church event to take place was the 'Flower and Egg' service. Collections on the day were for the Sunday School fund. The eggs and flowers were sent to the Whitehaven Infirmary.

The Girls Friendly Society was another social group. They held whist drives, and socials, to raise funds to help their work in the parish.

Church Choir - Miss Ives is the lady on the extreme left of the picture

World War One Prisoner of War Camp

During the First World War there was a German prisoner of war camp just beyond Kirkland School on the road to Salter. The South Wales Border Regiment was in charge of the camp.

Two of the guards were excellent singers and joined Lamplugh Church choir under the leadership of Mr Hales. They were Sergeant Price and Lieutenant Frederick Smallman Tew, who was in the Intelligence Corps and attached to the camp as an interpreter.

The camp was a mixture of tents and Nissen huts. The prisoners were sent out to work in the local quarries and on the nearby farms. Guards were sent out with the prisoners but if they were trustworthy they were left to get on with their work. One prisoner in particular was sent to work at Rowrah Hall Farm for the Watsons, and became firm family friend. After his return to Germany at the end of the war he continued to correspond until his death.

The prisoners, in their spare time, used to craft articles. They carved objects from the bones used in the preparation of their food. They made jewellery from silver paper which they melted down and moulded into brooches and rings, using stones found in the quarry as decoration. They also made wooden boxes, the tops inlayed with different coloured wood to make flowered patterns.

Some of the prisoners died in a flu epidemic and were buried in Lamplugh churchyard and St Joseph's churchyard in Frizington. Their bodies were exhumed in the mid 20th century and interred in a military cemetery.

Ring made for Bob Watson of Rowrah Hall Farm by German prisoner of war.

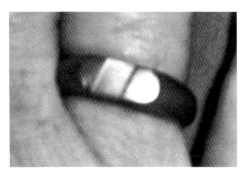

Some More First World War Memories

Irving McKenzie with his company

Irving McKenzie

Ted Blacklock and Johnny McCreadie, Border Regiment

Death Medal

Janie Gilmore from Arlecdon

Jane Newton Gilmore (Janie) was seven years old when her father, Thomas Gilmore, was crushed to death at Rowrah Head Quarry on 6th March 1914, whilst carrying out his duties as a Shot Firer. Janie was walking home from school when she overheard two neighbours talking. One said: "That bairn's father has just been killed in the quarry". Hearing of her father's death in this manner stayed with Janie for the rest of her life. Janie's eldest brother Will was eleven and her older brother Jim was ten. Her mother Mary Jane Gilmore (nee Dixon) was expecting another child, Tom, who was born 6 weeks after the tragic accident.

Thomas and Mary Jane had been married almost thirteen years. Their firstborn son, John Colville, lived only a few months and Janie's twin sister, Isabella Colville, died whilst having a fit at the age of 2 months in January 1907. Janie also took fits but her 'Granny Dixon' cured her of them at about 3mths of age by giving her a large dose of brandy and she had no more fits! (Janie swore that was why she did not like spirits)

According to the West Cumberland Times of Wednesday March 11th 1914, the funeral of Thomas Gilmore was one of the largest seen for many years, with people present from Workington, Whitehaven, Cockermouth, Brigham, Cleator Moor and the surrounding district. Tom Gilmore was a family man, a devout Christian and a prominent member of the Wesleyan Chapel in Rowrah. He was a Sunday School Teacher and leader of the Young Men's Class. It was said of him, that he was of a kind and generous nature, and was ready to help in any good cause. The Coroner at the Inquest into his death said it would be of some consolation to the widow and family to know how he was valued in the district.

Mary Jane received many letters at the time of her husband's death including those from Lizzie and Joe Shackley (Tom Gilmore's sister and her husband) who had emigrated to Canada, William Cowen, Secretary of the Cumberland Limestone Quarrymen's Association, Harold Bullough of Yorkshire who had been a Methodist Minister at Rowrah (I think), local people, and Harold Strathearn, of New York U.S.A who had previously been an evangelist in the village. (Not a happy time for Mr Strathearn, who says in his letter how much he appreciated Tom Gilmore's support in difficult circumstances).

Life was hard for Mary Jane Gilmore, (as it was for lots of women of her time), after the death of her husband. She opened a shop in her front room selling newspapers and home made bread, continuing to do this until the strike of 1927 when she found getting her money in increasingly difficult, so she closed the shop. She then became the local midwife, following in her mother's footsteps, at one time having brought into the world 75% of the babies in the area.

Janie's brother Will had to leave school soon after the death of his father to earn money to help keep the family, working at the Rowrah Railway Station. Her brother Jim was quite a scholar and was one of the first boys to go to the Whitehaven Grammar School from Arlecdon School. Jim later went to work as a boiler/fireman at Salter Head quarry where his Uncle, James Gilmore, was quarry manager. Janie went into service in Whitehaven, working for Dr Ablett and Mr & Mrs Kessel. Janie's youngest brother Tom's first job was driving a pony at Rowrah Head quarry where his father had lost his life.

Wedding of Jane Gilmore to Fred Seagrave February 1933 at Rowrah Methodist Church. L to R:- Sarah Cockbain, Bill Cockbain, Fred Seagrave, Jane Gilmore, Tom Gilmore and Janie Mason. Pictured below L to R: - Tom Gilmore, Mary Jane Gilmore, Bill Gilmore, Jane Seagrave nee Gilmore and Jim Gilmore

Thomas Gilmore Senior was the second youngest son of John and Isabella Gilmore who had come over from Ireland in 1861 with their eldest son James. John and Isabella went on to have five girls, including one set of twins and three more boys after settling firstly in Cockermouth and then Brigham at the Bread & Beer House. After the death of John, Isabella and her two youngest children, Tom & William moved to Arlecdon and in the 1901 census were living at 18 Rowrah Road Arlecdon.

On June 12th 1901 Thomas Gilmore married Mary Jane Dixon daughter of William and Jane Dixon of Arlecdon at Arlecdon Church.

Janie's maternal grandparents William and Jane (nee Newton) Dixon married on 15th January 1862. They lived at Mockerkin, Moor Howe and Asby before moving to Arlecdon in 1879 where Mary Jane and her younger sister Elizabeth Ann were born. By 1868 William had changed his occupation from a husbandman to a miner. William and Jane also had eight sons, one died in infancy, most of whom were coal miners or iron ore miners and lived in Arlecdon, Rowrah or Frizington. Mary Jane went into service and just before her marriage was employed by the Anderson's at the Stork Hotel, Rowrah. Elizabeth Ann became a pupil teacher at Arlecdon School.

To return to Janie Gilmore, she married Frederick William Seagrave on 23rd February 1933 at Rowrah Methodist Church. Fred was a quarryman and was well regarded by William Watson who was quarry manager at various quarries in the Arlecdon area. In the early 1930s during the slump years Fred moved to Penrith looking for work. He found work as a quarryman and shot firer with Harrison's Lime works at Flusco, near Penrith and so he and Janie were able to get married. They later moved to Shap where Fred became assistant manager at Shap Beck Lime Works.

Fred Seagrave was born in Workington in November 1906. He came to live in Arlecdon with his grandmother and step grandfather, Sarah and Thomas Jewess, attended Arlecdon School, sitting quite close to Janie, and was good friends with her three brothers all his life. Fred's mother and stepfather, Ada and Ernest Cockbain lived in Rowrah as did his half brother, Bill and half sister Sarah. He and the Gilmore brothers as well as Bill Cockbain were St John's Ambulance men and took part in lots of competitions, winning many medals. Fred continued to use his first aid skills all his working life, being responsible for first aid in the quarry at Shap Beck. Janie and Fred had three children, Thomas Gilmore who lived only one week, Dorothy Muriel and Mary Patricia, the writer of this article.

Contributed by Pat Newsham nee Seagrave

An interesting will of 1915

As recently as the early 20th Century, the members of the clergy were still called upon to write and witness wills for their parishioners. One such will makes interesting reading and follows the pattern of the earlier yeoman farmers by itemising specific articles and carefully naming the recipients. Jane Robinson, whose will this is, appeared to have been the owner of many valuable pieces, including wrestling belts and a silver tea and coffee service. Her use of 'her mark' instead of a signature also illustrates the fact that she was unable to write.

This is the last Will and Testament of Jane Robinson, widow of Dub Hall, Arlecdon, in the County of Cumberland. I hereby revoke all wills by me at any time heretofore made. I appoint Robert Henry Richardson of Low Asby, Arlecdon, and Cumberland to be my executor and direct that all my just debts and Funeral expenses shall be paid as soon as convenient after my decease.

I give and bequeath to my son, Robert Barnes Robinson, the sum of ten pounds, to my son George Barnes Robinson, the sum of ten pounds, to my son, William Wilson Robinson, the sum of ten pounds, to my daughter, Margaret Ann Richardson, the sum of ten pounds, to my daughter Sarah Warbrick, the sum of ten pounds.

I also give and bequeath one wrestling belt to my son, William, one wrestling belt to my son, John, one wresting belt to my son, Walker, the sewing machine to my daughter, Sarah, the kitchen fender to my son, William, the silver tea and coffee service to my son, Walker, the gold watch to my son, John, the gold chain in equal parts to my daughters, Margaret Ann and Sarah, the mahogany four- post bedstead to my daughter, Margaret Ann, the chest of drawers to my daughter, Sarah, one feather bed to my daughter Margaret Ann and one feather bed to my daughter Sarah; and the residue of my estate I give and bequeath in equal shares to my two sons John Robinson and Walker Robinson, In witness whereof I have hereunto set my hand this twenty first day of August one thousand nine hundred and fifteen.

Jane Robinson

 (her mark)

Signed with her mark by the above named testatrix as her last will and testament, the same having been first read out to her in the presence of us both present at the same time, who at her request,in her presence, and in the presence of each other have hereunto subscribed our names as witnesses.

H Hunter Parker, Clerk in Holy Orders
William Taylor Low Asby, Arlecdon, Cumberland

Jane died at Low Asby in 1921, aged 68, some years after making her will and is buried in Arlecdon Churchyard with her husband Thomas, who died in 1911.

1920 to 1929

Arlecdon War Memorial

At the end of the First World War 1914-1918 the people of Arlecdon erected a War Memorial in St Michael's Parish Churchyard, to honour the local servicemen who were killed in action.

The monument was designed by James Martindale and erected by Mr T Preston at the cost of £170. It was made of Cumberland red sand stone, composed of seven pieces, three of which form the base and four parts form the column. It has a Roman mosaic cross and is inscribed, 'In proud and loving memory' and the names of the fallen.

The Dedication Service and unveiling was on St Michael's Day Friday 22nd September 1922. The service was conducted in St Michael's Church by the Rural Dean, the Rev H. H. Parker and an address was given by the Lord Bishop of Carlisle. There was a large gathering of relations and friends of the fallen, ex-servicemen, public representatives, and vicars from local churches.

After the service the congregation proceeded to the War Memorial where Lieutenant Colonel Dixon from St Bees carried out the unveiling. The Bishop then dedicated the Memorial and floral tributes were laid at the foot of the column. Bugler Telford sounded the 'Last Post' and the 'Reveille'. Those present at the unveiling included Mr J. Dixon J.P., members of the Arlecdon and Frizington Council, the police and members of the Parochial Church Council.

Arlecdon Makes History

In an Act of Parliament in 1894 the Arlecdon and Frizington Urban District Council was formed. The Parish was divided into two wards with Arlecdon having three representatives and Frizington, having the greater population at the time, had six. They held their meetings in the prestigious Council Chambers, built in 1898 at a cost of £1500, on the Main Street, Frizington. The members were mainly Liberals and Conservatives until in 1919, John Jackson Adams, an Arlecdon man, having recently returned from New Zealand, persuaded eight local men to stand for election to the council under the Socialist banner. They campaigned with great enthusiasm and were duly elected to form **the first all Labour local government body in the country** with Jack Adams as chairman and Walter Hocking, vice-chairman.

Their progress is recorded in an article in The Evening News and Star of Friday July 8th 1983 by Frank Carruthers, from which the following extracts are taken.

"The eyes of the country are on Arlecdon and Frizington" said Tom Cape, M.P. for Workington, "the first all Labour council in the kingdom."

The vicar invited the new councillors to attend a service to ask God's blessing on the work of the council but some of the members thought they could manage without it! However, it was put to the vote and it was decided by a single vote to accept the invitation.

The council began by giving all council employees a holiday for May Day. They also reduced their working week to 44 hours and put up their wages. According to Jack Adams, they were the only authority in England able to pay its road sweepers four guineas a week!

With a rateable value of £33,000, Arlecdon and Frizington was one of the wealthiest urban districts in Cumberland. To raise money for a maternity and child welfare centre, Jack Adams proposed that the iron ore mines be re-rated. He maintained that the current rating was "the most colossal swindle that had ever taken place," and he accused the County Council's Assessment Committee of being influenced by the mine and royalty owners.

They set about house owners to improve their properties and ordered the sanitary inspector to come down heavily on the 21 owners of the 175 houses needing improvement. They sacked the then Medical Officer, with whom Jack Adams had had previous clashes, because he asked for a rise in salary and then proceeded to employ a new M.O.H at double the salary of the old.

By this time the iron industry was falling into decline with cheaper ore being shipped into the country from Spain. This made it difficult to persuade the authorities to increase the assessment on the local mines, but Jack Adams and his U.D.C. took it upon themselves to increase the rates by sixpence in the pound. Three-pence of that rise was used to provide the West's first recreation ground for children, two-pence to provide jobs for two ex-soldiers in road work and a penny in the pound for further education. Apparently, this last penny was never spent as no-one got round to organising any classes.

The council then set out to build the first new council houses in Cumberland.
(Probably at Lingla Bank)

But their luck was to change with decline of the iron and coal industries. Miners were asked to take pay cuts and there were many strikes. When industrial experts were sent into the area to try and find out the reasons for the unrest they found only a single blast furnace working at Workington and no-one working in the iron-ore mines which had until recently employed 8,000 men.

Unemployment was rife and the voters took it out on Arlecdon and Frizington's dynamic Labour local government by voting Labour out of power in the 1922 election.

In 1934 the Urban District Council was absorbed into the Ennerdale Rural District Council, which, in turn, in 1972 became part of Copeland Borough Council.

Jack Adams went on to become a County Alderman and magistrate. In the 1930s he became General Manager of the West Cumberland Development Company and was responsible for bringing new industries, such as Marchon, to what was then, a very depressed area.

He was awarded the OBE in 1948 and received an honorary degree from Durham University, became a Freeman of the Boroughs of Whitehaven and Workington and was made a Baron in the New Years Honours list January 1st 1949 when he became Lord Adams of Ennerdale.

He died in 1960 and his ashes are interred in Arlecdon churchyard, marked by a simple headstone close to the west tower.

The Adams Hall in the village is named after John Jackson Adams - a political pioneer.

Arlecdon & Frizington Public Representatives, 1919
Standing (left to right) – J. Dixon UDC, W. Watson UDC, R. Spiers UDC, J. Walsh UDC, PLG,
E. L. Robinson UDC, A. Spedding UDC and T. Cape MP.
Seated – W. Hocking, Vice Chairman UDC, F. Hodges, J. J. Adams CC, JP, Chairman, UDC,
R. Smillie, H. Crellin PLC

Rowrah YMCA

As the population of the parish increased, there was a need for recreational facilities for the young people and so the YMCA was opened by one of Queen Victoria's daughters in the early 1900s. It provided a reading room, tennis courts, billiards, cricket and the opportunity for further education through lectures and the very popular Debating Society.

Outings were organised by the Secretary Fletcher Watson.

Jon Henley was a member of the Rowrah YMCA Cricket Club and among his papers, after his death in 1964, was an old Club Score Book (now in Whitehaven Record Office). He left Cumberland to pursue a very successful career in local government. He was clerk to Frizington, Whitehaven and Ennerdale Rural District Councils before moving to Whiston, Merseyside to take up a similar position.

William, Joseph and Fletcher were the brothers of Mary Martha Henley and a cousin of James. It would appear that the Debating Society was very much a Watson family affair!

The YMCA Debating and Literary Society at Buttermere 1926

Photo by T Horsley, Lamplugh. Back row L to R: - NK, NK, James Watson, Jonathan Watson (father of James), Mr Kirkbride, NK. Next Row: - ? Mr Pritt, Fletcher Watson (Secretary), Joseph Watson, NK, Jon Henley, William Watson. Next Row: - NK, NK. Front Row: - NK, NK, Lizzie Watson (wife of Joseph), Miss Sweeten (school teacher, later to become Mrs Crosthwaite), NK, Sally Watson (wife of William), Martha Mary Henley (wife of Jon, nee Watson)

Thomas Richards

A Family Firm

In years gone by, long obituaries appeared in the local press which gave detailed accounts of funeral services, the clergymen who conducted them, the names of those who sent flowers and tributes, the hymns that were sung, facts about the deceased person's life and work and the names of family members in attendance – great stuff for family historians.

One such obituary in a local newspaper in 1924 tells us of the life of a lady named Ann Richards the wife of Thomas Richards who came to Cumberland from Cornwall like many of his fellow countrymen to work in the mines. On his journey north in the 1870s, Thomas spent some time in Wales where he met and married Ann.

Thomas was employed by the Asby Colliery Company but in his spare time he travelled the country districts selling drapery. Ann was a talented dressmaker and milliner and their products were much in demand from the ever growing population of the area.

So successful was their enterprise that they eventually moved to Frizington and opened a large and substantial drapery, hardware and furniture shop.

However, this was only the beginning. More shops were established in Cleator Moor, Millom, Maryport, Aspatria and Broughton in Furness and as their family grew up (there were six sons and three daughters), they and their respective spouses were installed as managers.

The Dalton-in-Furness shop with Edwin Richards standing in the doorway

Sadly, their youngest son Edward, who managed the Dalton in Furness shop, was killed in the final days of the First World War aged 29 years. He is buried in a cemetery in Denain but his name is recorded on the family tombstone in Arlecdon Churchyard along with his parents and his sister Beatrice.

Thomas's commercial enterprises didn't take up all of his energies. He supported the Liberal party and was Chairman of the Arlecdon and Frizington Urban Council. He took a keen interest in education and sat on the Arlecdon and Weddicar School Board. He was also a Methodist Local Preacher.

Thomas died on a return visit to his native Falmouth in 1923 aged 75 years and was buried there alongside one of his daughters, Beatrice, who died on August 15th 1908 aged 21 years. She had been taken to Cornwall by her father to find out if the milder climate could improve her failing health.

Less than a year after her husband's death, Ann, who had always maintained good health and remained very active, contracted a chill and despite the efforts of Dr Quine, developed pneumonia which led to her death at the home of her daughter, Mrs Pearce, on the 23rd January 1924 in her 73rd year.

Her funeral reflected the esteem in which she was held by the local community. After a part of the funeral service was conducted in the home of her daughter in Frizington, eight motor cars followed the hearse to Arlecdon Churchyard where the Committal was carried out by the Rev. H. Wright, Primitive Methodist Superintendent of the Whitehaven Circuit.

There were many floral tributes including those from her son, John, in Vancouver B.C. and her daughter, Clara, in New Zealand.

One of Mrs Richard's daughters married a Mr F Moon and ran her parent's shop under that name for many years.

Her youngest daughter, Florence May, married Mr J. J. Pearce, agent for the Prudential Insurance Company. They had a daughter, Olive, and a son, Raymond, who so kindly provided this information about the family.

Ann Richards with daughter Florence May outside lych gate at Arlecdon Church

Mrs Pearce driving a Model T Ford with the Moon family on board

1930 to 1939

Life on the Farm in the 1930s

Margaret Bell

Memories from Margaret Bell

At the bottom of Arlecdon Road in the village of Arlecdon is Spittal Square, a group of farmhouses. After the death of the owner Mr J Spittal on 31st May 1914 the estate went to probate and eventually two of the farms and a cottage were sold in 1921 for £1500 together with 81 acres to William Jackson of Low Leys, Lamplugh. Upon the marriage of one of their daughters to Mr Gill, Mrs Jackson gave Arlecdon Farm and Alexandra Cottage to them as a wedding present. They had six children, Berry, William, Harold, Wilfred, Jackson and Ann. Upon the death of Mr Gill in 1929, Mrs Mary Ponsonby Gill moved with all the family into her parent's home at Hakodadi, a substantial property on Arlecdon Low Road, to live with her mother Elizabeth Jackson.

At this time Margaret Bell's (nee Bowness) parents were farming Low Arlecdon Farm, (now called Arlecdon Howe Farm). On the 2nd February 1929 they moved onto Arlecdon Farm, Candlemass being the official moving day for farms, renting the farm from Mrs Gill. Margaret's Aunty and Uncle moved into Low Arlecdon Farm (the Irving's) with their children, Dorothy, John, Joan, William, Margaret, Amy and Sarah. After the Irving's father died the farm was then rented by Mrs Gill to Mr Rawlins.

Margaret's parents had four children, Mary, Joseph (Joe), Margaret and Thomas who died as a child of flu. Margaret's mother died on 23rd March 1929. Their Aunty Annie came to live at the farm to bring up the family. Mr Bowness hired a man and a lad to help around the farm, they lived in one of the rooms at the back of the farmhouse. For the house, a young servant girl was employed. She also lived in one of the back rooms of the farmhouse.

The hired servant girl usually took up this sort of position at the age of 14 just after leaving school. One she remembers, Nellie Troughton, stayed with them for quite some time, she made the beds, made meals, baked, scrubbed floors, cleaned the house, made up the fires, did the washing and bathed the children in the tin bath. When it was a wet or snowy day Margaret would stay at school for lunch, the servant girl would be sent up the road to Arlecdon School to take the children's lunch.

The servant girls were hired on a 6 months contract, the hiring days were in Spring and Autumn. An advert was placed in the paper and they received £9 - £10 for the six months plus their keep for the term. A lot were kept on and some stayed with the family for many years. After Margaret left school the servants were no longer required as the girls took over their chores but the hired lad was kept on to do hand and wheel barrow work etc.

At this time on the farm the cows they kept produced milk to make butter and cream. The Bowness's had lots of customers for their butter which they sold at 1 shilling per lb. They had a vegetable patch and grew carrots, turnip, cauliflower, cabbage and beetroot. They had their own hens, set their own eggs, got pullets (young hens) and cockerels. The cockerels made a nice roast chicken for dinner. They usually reared geese for Christmas and also kept ducks.

In 1939 Mr Bowness, Margaret's father, was injured and knocked over whilst watering his bull. He spent approximately one month in Whitehaven's hospital 'Castle Hospital'. To visit, the family caught the bus from Arlecdon; they ran every half hour in those days.

During the war they were allowed to kill and cure two pigs per year which they made bacon, ham, lard, sausage and black pudding. As there were no freezing facilities Margaret's Aunty would bottle potted meat and pig's liver. Only the older pigs were slaughtered. The young pigs were fed on potato peelings, cabbage leaves etc. They had hot water from two set pots, one for their use and one to boil the corn for the horses and pig potatoes for the pigs. Their coal came by horse and cart from Station House, Arlecdon.

Jumpers and socks were knitted with thick wool, Margaret's dad wore clogs. Aunty Annie was a good seamstress and made a lot of their clothes. Margaret wore a navy blue gym slip and pinafore with black socks and garters. She wore clogs on her feet for school. It cost ½d for a small caulker and 1d for a big caulker to repair the clogs. Once Margaret had left school she wore a corset to keep her stockings up.

What they could not grow on the farm they had to buy. Flour was bought in 5 and 10 stone bags at Rowrah Co-op, sugar, salt in oblong wedges two feet long. The salt was used to make the butter every week. Miss Edmonds was in charge of the drapery department where towelling and materials could be purchased.

Arlecdon Farmhouse

Sunday School played a very big part in the family for the children. They went to Arlecdon Sunday School each Sunday afternoon for one hour, reading parts out of the Bible, and prayers and also learning their Catechism. She had to say her prayers every night "Gentle Jesus meek and mild look upon a little child, pity my simplicity, teach me Lord to come to Thee, God bless Mammy, Daddy, Bothers and Sisters".

Once a year Margaret went on her Sunday School trip, she was given a food bag, teacake, cake and sandwich. She remembers going to Seascale and buying a teapot from the shop there. They caught the train from Winder Station. School trips started about 1936 up until the war. She remembers going to Glasgow one year and Edinburgh to see the Castle and visit the Zoo another year. She paid 6d (2½p) per week into a fund at school to be able to afford to go.

In the early 1930s Mr & Mrs Robinson lived next door in Alexandra Cottage with their children Tom, Joseph, George, Walker and Eleanor. They rented this cottage from Mrs Gill. In 1936 Mr and Mrs Douglas rented Alexandra Cottage. They had no children but in later years were 'Aunty and Uncle' to Margaret's children.

In Mr Douglas's garden he grew potatoes, green peas, lettuce, shallots, rhubarb and radishes. In his green house he grew tomatoes, chrysanthemums to sell. He kept a few hens. He first kept them in the old quarry below Arlecdon Farm and went twice a day to feed them. He then built his black shed at the side of the barn and kept them in there. He kept a pig in the 'coal house'. Lots of people kept a pig and fed them on their scraps. Mrs Douglas worked as a washer woman for Mrs Gill – she went there every Monday. Mr Harry Simon from Arlecdon House helped Mr Douglas to put in a large Edwardian second hand bath into the Cottage.

Though there was no electricity, TV etc., the family listened to the radio which ran on wet batteries. Mr Jackson from Frizington came every week to re-charge them. "We were never bored; we played cards, dominos, and board games, the girls knitted jumpers and played out around the farm".

Prior to electricity 1958/9 oil lamps were used. A water toilet was installed in 1964, paid for by Mrs Gill, (water and toilet). Prior to this the toilet was a dry toilet outside up the yard, the soil being disposed of over the land prior to a chemical toilet being installed. Next door at Alexandra Cottage the soil was collected by horse and cart to be taken away as they did not have the land on which to dispose it.

Today Margaret still lives in the family farmhouse at Arlecdon Farm, her family having bought it in 1976 when it came up for sale after the death of Mrs Mary Ponsonby Gill. Up until recently Margaret kept hens. Today one of her daughters and her son live near to her, her other daughter living away and she takes great pleasure from her grandchildren. She still has many old long standing friends in the village and further afield whom she visits and who come to visit her.

My Grandmother

Jennifer Carruthers

My grandmother, Jane, was always called Jinny and was born at Middle Leys, Lamplugh, in 1899. She was the 5th daughter of Mary Jane and Thomas Mavir. Thomas was a quarryman, and worked at Rowrah Quarry. In 1900 they moved to Lamplugh Cross, where they had a small grocers shop.

Their 6th daughter Lily was born there in 1901. They lived very near to the 'Lamplugh Arms' public house, and being Methodists did not believe in drinking alcohol. The men going in the shop used to tease Jane about going for a drink. Jane said that she would never cross the threshold of a public house. One day on going to collect baby Lily, after leaving her outside in her sleeping basket, Jane discovered that she and the basket were missing, so she went into the pub frantically hoping someone had seen something. There they all were with Lily, laughing, saying that they knew that this would fetch her to where she said she would never go. It all turned out well. Jane saw the funny-side and Lily was safely returned and the men had put money in the crib for the baby.

The field out the back was used for 'serving' mares. The stallion, known as 'The Entire', was brought round the villages to serve the mares. When this was happening, Jane brought the children in and closed the curtains until the deed was done. Then they were allowed to go back outside to play!

The family moved to Arlecdon and the girls went to school there. One day when going to school, some men were waiting to go to work asked my grandmother what she was called, on replying Jinny, one man said "Nay lass, thou can't be called Jinny, that's a hosses' name!"

On leaving school Jinny went into service, working as a housemaid at Lingmel at Seascale. She liked her work, and the 'gentry' she worked for. She was paid one shilling a week (5p) and, of course, her keep, as she had to live in. She sent her mother sixpence (2½p) each week and came home on her day off. The servants were well fed and were allowed anything they wanted to eat. The only thing Jinny wouldn't eat was the game that was hung until the 'mowks' were dropping off it. They were allowed a couple of hours off work every Sunday to go to Chapel and a short walk.

Her friend Belle Holiday worked in the kitchen. She used to cook breakfast for the 'gentry' giving them their favourite fried bananas. Belle used to say, "I don't know what you think these look like, but to me they looked like "sh... with sugar on!"

They used to sneak out to go to dances at Santon Bridge and Seascale and the old cook would leave the window open for them to get back in.

Jinny married Irving McKenzie and lived first at Frizington where four of her five children were born, Joan, Irving, Margaret, and Sarah. Irving was born with a large tumour behind his ear. The doctor said that when he came the next day he would operate if Grandma Mavir would assist him. Grandma Mavir used to go around nursing the sick, sitting with people who were dying and delivering babies. The doctor would call on her as there were no district nurses in those days. The doctor came the next day, and Irving had the operation on the kitchen table and the tumour was successfully removed.

Alexandra Cottage

Alexandra Cottage Low Arlecdon

Mr & Mrs Douglas 1937 - 1996

Mr Stanley and Mrs Ethel Nicholson Douglas became tenants of Alexandra Cottage renting the property off Mrs Elizabeth Jackson of Hakodadi on the 7th September 1937, four years after they were married. Stan had met Ethel by chance in 1931 near Birks Farm, Cleator Moor, where Ethel was pushing her bicycle because of a burst tyre. Stan quickly mended the puncture, love blossomed and two years later they were married at St Michael's Church, Arlecdon.

Mr Douglas was born at Birks Cottage, Cleator Moor having an older brother called John Douglas and a sister Annie Steel who in the 1980s lived at Birks Farm, Cleator Moor. Over the years Mr Douglas was employed by Cumberland Motor Services as a handyman and driver, but in his younger days he experienced the rigours of outdoor life as a quarryman, working limestone at Rowrah, Deanscales and Clints Egremont.

Mrs Douglas (nee Goggins) hailed from Winder, Frizington, one of 13 children, but by the 1980s only one brother was still living. Mrs Douglas was not only christened at St Michael's Church but was confirmed there. She worked for Mrs Gill at Hakodadi.

They did not have any children of their own but were very close to Margaret Bell's children, from Arlecdon Farm.

Mr Douglas (Stan) was well known in the village for his garden. This was his main passion. His display of Lupins in his front garden was well known locally. Many of his neighbours would walk down the hill from the village to admire his colourful display. In his back garden he grew a variety of vegetables and fruit, he kept hens in a black shed which was at the side

Mr Douglas's Lupins

of the barn and had been know to keep a pig in one of the outbuildings. Besides tendering his own garden he also kept things in good trim at Arlecdon House for Mr and Mrs Simon.

On the 12th December 1955 Mrs Elizabeth Jackson died leaving Alexandra Cottage to her daughter Mrs Mary Ponsonby Gill. Mr & Mrs Douglas bought the cottage from Mrs Gill on 5th June 1956 paying the princely sum of £125.00. In December 1959 they employed Mr Henry Nevinson, joiner of 2 Rowrah Road, Rowrah, to replace certain windows, front door and construct a front porch. In 1961 Mr Nevinson replaced the wooden floor in the main bedroom. The privy was outside around the back of the barn; however they did have a bathroom with a sink and huge Edwardian bath. The hot water for the bathroom and kitchen was provided by a back boiler behind the fire in their living room. In their little sitting room there was a slate fireplace which was decorated to look like wood. Both these items were saved and retained in the cottage when it was renovated by the new owners in 1997/8.

In September 1981 Stan and Ethel celebrated their 50th Golden Wedding Anniversary with a small party for family and friends in their cottage. Mrs Douglas died on the 29th October 1985 followed 11 years later by Mr Douglas in April 1996. They had both lived very happy lives in their little cottage at Arlecdon having felt that all that they wanted was near to hand, good neighbours, a comfortable home, a lovely garden and a pub, the Sun Inn, within walking distance for Stan to enjoy his pint.

W. Spear and engine at Dean Moor

Death of Mr G W Thomas
Managing Director of Dean Moor Colliery, March 16th 1931

A measure of the esteem in which Mr Thomas was held was illustrated by the number of people who attended his funeral. Over 1,000 people gathered for the service and the combined brass bands of St Paul's and St Joseph's played the hymn, 'Peace Perfect Peace'.

Mr Thomas was, at one time, the only employer of labour in Arlecdon Parish and was highly respected by his workmen.

His daughter, Mary Harper, was the mother of Gerald Harper, the actor. The family spent their holidays in the area and called their house in London, 'Frizington'.

There are references to coal being mined at Dean Moor from the mid 19th century to its closure in the mid 20th century.

According to information in the Durham Mining Museum Archives, the following were among those killed at the colliery: -

Foster William, 13 Aug 1902, aged 29, Hewer, while hewing in a longwall working in the Anthony or Two Feet seam, a false bedded stone fell from the roof canting out two props which were set under the thin edge ; the stone was 9 feet long by 3½ feet wide with a thickness of 6 to 11 inches, and came away at a greasy parting when the deceased had taken out the supporting coal

Hutchinson Peter, 08 Jun 1912, aged 30, Miner, whilst working in a stone drift that had just reached the coal seam, an influx of water from old workings came away

Smith Joseph, 06 Apr 1881, aged 15, Putter, killed by a fall of stone

Tear Thomas, 24 Dec 1910, aged 41, Hewer, fall of stone at working place

Thompson W., 10 Oct 1889, aged 50, Hewer, crushed by tubs

Dancing and Dance Bands

June Tucker

One of the favourite evening activities for Arlecdon folk in the 1930s and 1940s was dancing. These dances used to take place in Haggerty's Barn, Arlecdon and the WI Hall in Lamplugh.

Several bands used to play at these dances including Billy Bowman's with Florrie on piano. Also Mitcheson's with Jimmy on drums and Joe on accordion. The Blue Rockets were also very popular. The Ambassadors were regular entertainers with Stan McNamara on fiddle, Tommy Moore on trumpet, Erin Coates on drums and Ivan McNamara piano, vocals and saxophone.

People walked, biked, got a lift with Albert Bitcon in his Austin 7 or with Erin Jefferson or with Sammy Davidson who drove the taxi for the Ambassadors. Even after a hard day's work on the farm, in the pit or factory, everyone made the effort to go dancing on Friday and Saturday nights.

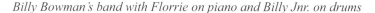

Billy Bowman's band with Florrie on piano and Billy Jnr. on drums

1940 to 1949

The Second World War 1939-1945

It is not known how many men and women from Arlecdon enlisted to serve in the forces during the Second World War 1939-1945. The names of the men killed in action are inscribed on the war memorial in St. Michael's Churchyard, Arlecdon.

The Seven Men Killed

Private William Briggs aged 29, South Lancashire Regiment, died 14th June 1944, buried La Delivrande War Cemetery Doures.

Aircraftman Donald Robert Brown aged 28, Royal Air Service Volunteer, son of Robert and Amy Brown, husband of Mary, died 2nd July 1942, buried at St Michael's Churchyard Arlecdon.

Private John Young Charlton aged 19, Monmouthshire Regiment, son of John Young Charlton and Eleanor of Winder, died 2nd December 1944, buried Swartbroek Churchyard.

William Tyson Gill aged 21, Royal Artillery, son of Robert and Mary P. Gill, died 30th March 1943. Memorial Medjez-el-Bab Tunisia.

Sergeant John Watson Leathes aged 31, Royal Artillery, son of Joseph Fox Leathes and Sarah, died 1st November 1944, buried Kirkee War Cementary India.

Sergeant Wilfred Ray, aged 22, Royal Air Force Volunteer Reserve, son of James and Florence Ray, died 19th July 1944, buried Sailly-Flibean Aucourt Churchyard, France.

Robinson Stables aged 21, Royal Air Force Volunteer Reserve, son of Edward and Annie Stables, died 22nd December 1942, buried St Michaels's Churchyard.

Second World War Memories

John Irving was born in 1924 at Arlecdon. In his youth he lived with his family (seven children in all) at Routensyke Farm then Low Arlecdon Farm, attending Arlecdon School. After his father died in 1940, the family moved across the road into a house that his parents had bought prior to the father's death.

Prior to being called up to serve in the Second World War John Irving left school at 13 initially working on his father's farm then was employed by Davidson's of St Bees as a rigger, boring holes looking for coal and iron ore. He received his Call Up papers to serve

John Irving 1940

William Briggs and Lenny Seward

in the army in 1942 at the age of 18. He had six weeks to adjust to the idea of joining. Notification came to say that he would firstly be sent to Blachin, Chester for his 12 week basic training. Upon the completion of his basic training he was then transferred to Sicily with the Royal Engineer Regiment to helping to build Pontoon Bridges, Bailey Bridges and lifting land mines. This was a far cry from the life he had known in Arlecdon.

Throughout his time in the army he was transferred between different divisions, wherever he was required. Initially the Armoured Division, then was moved between the 78th Battle Division and the 56th Black Cats Division. He travelled through Italy, Austria, Germany and France. On the 26th August 1943 he became ill and was diagnosed with Appendicitis. The army transferred him to the 97th General Field Hospital in Tunisia on 13th September 1943 where he underwent an Appendectomy. He remained in this hospital for three months. Upon being discharged he returned to his division in Italy.

The Germans not only bombed they also dropped propaganda leaflets trying to demoralise the troops and persuade them to surrender. John still has some of these leaflets in his memory box. He encountered many sad times when he witnessed the death of many of his colleagues but also had cheery times with the comradeship of the many friends he made.

While in Italy his platoon came across deserted farms where food and chickens had been left abandoned. This unexpected supply of food supplemented their rations. Vineyards had also been discarded and vats of wine left. When German troops were retreating, John and fellow soldiers came across a deserted German trench. The Germans had moved on so quickly that they had left behind a large ham shank which the troops thoroughly enjoyed eating.

When the end of war was declared John found himself in Italy repairing bridges over the River Po, boring for fresh water, renovating, repairing and painting-out large properties and repairing roads and the infrastructure. At this time they were allowed some leave. John took advantage of this and went skiing. The army entered him into a skiing competition at Cortina in Italy. They provided all the entrants with army regulation skiing equipment. John was entered into the Skimozzle race which he won, proudly receiving two medals.

He was not demobbed until 1947. He was paid 7s 6d (35.5p) per week. After discharge he was retained on the reserve list for active service for a number of years.

John's brother, William was called to active service in 1945 when he was 18. After his three months basic training in Lockerbie and Glasgow he was transferred to Palestine where he served for the rest of the war. He was demobbed in 1948.

Other Arlecdon men who were also called up were Joe Bell, Navy, Harold Gill, Navy, Joe Merritt, Navy, Jake Tyson, Air Force, Sam Troughton, Army. Jackie Richardson, Norman Kirkbride, Raymond Kirkbride (in India for his 21st birthday), James Tomlinson and Jackie Seward (serving in the Airforce). After the war Jackie emigrated to Australia but unfortunately died in a fire.

Lenny Seward was in the Home Guard, one of the Bevin Boys working in the pit. On the day of the 1947 William Pit disaster Lenny was asked to go with John and friends to Carlisle Races, however he was offered an extra shift, which proved fatal, as he was one of the victims of this terrible pit disaster.

Below, John relaxing with friends in Italy and as the Army skiing champion (above)

+28/3

NATIONAL SERVICE (ARMED FORCES) ACT, 1939
ENLISTMENT NOTICE

MINISTRY OF LABOUR AND NATIONAL SERVICE
EMPLOYMENT EXCHANGE,
QUAY ST.,
MANCHESTER

Posted at .... (place) on
.... (date) at .... (time)
with P.O. for 4s. *and travelling warrant.
.... (Sig.)
*Delete if not applicable. .... (Date)

Date — 13 JUL 1940

Mr. *David Holliday Woodward*
6 Pasture Rd.
Rowrah Workington Cumb.
Registration No. CKT 1118

YOU SHOULD TAKE
THIS NOTICE
WITH YOU WHEN
YOU REPORT

DEAR SIR,
In accordance with the National Service (Armed Forces) Act, 1939, you are called
upon for service in the .... TERRITORIAL ARMY ...... and are required to present yourself
between 9 a.m. and 12 noon
on *Thurs* day *18th July* 19 *40*, at 10 a.m., or as early
as possible thereafter on that day, to :— *Royal Artillery*
25th Medium + Heavy Training Regt.
Marske in Redcar
Marske ...... (nearest railway station).

A Travelling Warrant for your journey is enclosed. Before starting your journey you
must exchange the warrant for a ticket at the booking office named on the warrant. If
possible, this should be done a day or two before you are due to travel.
A Postal Order for 4s. in respect of advance of service pay, is also enclosed. Uniform
and personal kit will be issued to you after joining H.M. Forces. Any kit that you take with
you should not exceed an overcoat, change of clothes, stout pair of boots, and personal kit,
such as razor, hair brush, tooth brush, soap and towel.
Immediately on receipt of this notice, you should inform your employer of the date
upon which you are required to report for service.
Yours faithfully,
H. N. GRUNDY
Manager

THOMAS GILMORE

Among the last batch of British War Prisoners to be repatriated from Italy was Private Thomas Gilmore, son of Mary Jane and Thomas Gilmore of Rowrah. Tom enlisted in the Royal Army Medical Corps in 1939 and after undertaking his basic training in 1940 he was sent to the Middle East.

Tom was captured by the Germans in April 1941 and held prisoner of war in Tripoli until January 1942 and then transferred to Sicily until 1943. In June 1943 there was an exchange of prisoners of war to take place in Turkey. Tom with other prisoners of war was exchanged. He was allowed home by escorting a

David Woodward (standing)

Thomas Gilmore

fellow blind prisoner returning via Egypt and the Cape to England.

Tom spent his leave with his wife and 3 year old daughter before returning back to active service. Tom was a survivor of the Second World War.

War Work and A.T.S.

Army Training Service.

Joan McKenzie was called up to do war work in 1941 at the age of eighteen. She went to work at Fairies Aviation in Stockport, where she had to sit an examination and, coming out top, she was given the position of an inspector. Inspecting the riveting work on the aeroplane wings was one job she talked about saying that after sitting a tough exam she was given a spanner and a pencil. Then she was sent to check the riveting with the spanner, marking them appropriately with the pencil.

She left Fairies to go and join the A.T.S. in 1944 aged 21. She was stationed first in Redditch, Cheshire, then was transferred to Canterbury where she worked in the Pay Corps. She used a comptometer (the forerunner of today's computer) in her work. She remained with the A.T.S. until 1948.

Plane Crash

On the evening of the 25th March 1941, a V Wellington plane developed engine trouble and crash landed on the main road near Heather Lea, hitting the telephone wires.

The crew escaped uninjured and the pilot was lodged at the Anchor Hotel, Frizington. The plane was on a delivery flight from RAF Moreton-in-the-Marsh. It was watched over by the Home Guard until a salvage unit from RAF Silloth came to take it away, but even they were unable to prevent the crafty removal of Perspex from the cockpit, which was used to make rings for some lucky local girls.

Stan Huddart

Joan Mc Kenzie

Did you know?
John Scott of 'Hodcott' Arlecdon Road was awarded the George Medal

The Holmans – tragedy of a local family

The Holmans from Rheda Mansion, Frizington, a well known and respected family who attended St Michael's Church Arlecdon, were in their London home at Holland Villas Road during the first months of the 2nd World War when an air raid warning was given. The house received a direct hit by a German bomb, killing Alwyn Holman, aged 50, husband of Myfanwy Holman and their 17 year old daughter Benita Rosemary Joyce Holman. Other members of the family had a narrow escape.

The family had made plans to visit Devonshire before returning to Rheda. The bodies of father and daughter were cremated at Golders Green, London and their ashes were taken to Devonshire and scattered out at sea.

Mrs Holman was the daughter of Thomas Dixon, whose ancestors had lived at Rheda for many generations. She brought the rest of the family to Rheda for the duration of the war and later lived in the converted stable block, known as The Dower House, until her death in the 1970s.

Mrs Holman

Rheda Mansion, Frizington

A 1940s Double Wedding

Two Winder sisters, Annie and Lena Charlton, daughters of Mr and Mrs J Charlton, Station House, had a double wedding on Whit Monday. Annie, a sergeant in the W.A.A.F. married Lance Corporal Arthur Dixon. She wore a gown of pink satin beaute, with a wreath of orange blossom and veil. Her bridesmaid was Miss E Thompson. Lena married William Jackson and was dressed in gold satin beaute with a veil and coronet of orange blossom. Her bridesmaid was Miss L Jackson, sister of the groom.

On leaving the church the brides were presented with silver horse shoes by Grace Sloan and Eleanor Campbell

8th June, 1946

TO-DAY, AS WE CELEBRATE VICTORY, I send this personal message to you and all other boys and girls at school. For you have shared in the hardships and dangers of a total war and you have shared no less in the triumph of the Allied Nations.

I know you will always feel proud to belong to a country which was capable of such supreme effort; proud, too, of parents and elder brothers and sisters who by their courage, endurance and enterprise brought victory. May these qualities be yours as you grow up and join in the common effort to establish among the nations of the world unity and peace.

George R.I

IMPORTANT
WAR DATES

1939

SEP 1. Germany invaded Poland

SEP 3. Great Britain and France declared war on Germany; the B.E.F. began to leave for France

DEC 13. Battle of the River Plate

1940

APR 9. Germany invaded Denmark and Norway

MAY 10. Germany invaded the Low Countries

JUNE 3. Evacuation from Dunkirk completed

JUNE 8. British troops evacuated from Norway

JUNE 11. Italy declared war on Great Britain

JUNE 22. France capitulated

JUNE 29. Germans occupied the Channel Isles

AUG 8–OCT 31. German air offensive against Great Britain (Battle of Britain)

OCT 28. Italy invaded Greece

NOV 11–12. Successful attack on the Italian Fleet in Taranto Harbour.

DEC 9–11. Italian invasion of Egypt defeated at the battle of Sidi Barrani

1941

MAR 11. Lease-Lend Bill passed in U.S.A.

MAR 28. Battle of Cape Matapan

APR 6. Germany invaded Greece

APR 12–DEC 9. The Siege of Tobruk

MAY 20. Formal surrender of remnants of Italian Army in Abyssinia

MAY 20–31. Battle of Crete

MAY 27. German battleship *Bismarck* sunk

JUNE 22. Germany invaded Russia

AUG 12. Terms of the Atlantic Charter agreed

NOV 18. British offensive launched in the Western Desert

DEC 7. Japanese attacked Pearl Harbour

DEC 8. Great Britain and United States of America declared war on Japan

1942

FEB 15. Fall of Singapore

APR 16. George Cross awarded to Malta

OCT 23–NOV 4. German-Italian army defeated at El Alamein

NOV 8. British and American forces landed in North Africa

1943

JAN 31. The remnants of the 6th German Army surrendered at Stalingrad

MAY Final victory over the U-Boats in the Atlantic

MAY 13. Axis forces in Tunisia surrendered

JULY 10. Allies invaded Sicily

SEP 3. Allies invaded Italy

SEP 8. Italy capitulated

DEC 26. *Scharnhorst* sunk off North Cape

1944

JAN 22. Allied troops landed at Anzio

JUNE 4. Rome captured

JUNE 6. Allies landed in Normandy

JUNE 13. Flying-bomb (V.1) attack on Britain started

JUNE Defeat of Japanese invasion of India

AUG 25. Paris liberated

SEP 3. Brussels liberated

SEP 8. The first rocket-bomb (V.2) fell on England.

SEP 17–26. The Battle of Arnhem

OCT 20. The Americans re-landed in the Philippines

1945

JAN 17. Warsaw liberated

MAR 20. British recaptured Mandalay

MAR 23. British crossed the Rhine

APR 25. Opening of Conference of United Nations at San Francisco

MAY 2. German forces in Italy surrendered

MAY 3. Rangoon recaptured

MAY 5. All the German forces in Holland, N.W. Germany and Denmark surrendered unconditionally

MAY 9. Unconditional surrender of Germany to the Allies ratified in Berlin

JUNE 10. Australian troops landed in Borneo

AUG 6. First atomic bomb dropped on Hiroshima

AUG 8. Russia declared war on Japan

AUG 9. Second atomic bomb dropped on Nagasaki

AUG 14. The Emperor of Japan broadcast the unconditional surrender of his country

SEP 5. British forces re-entered Singapore

MY FAMILY'S WAR RECORD

Childhood Memories of the 1940s

By Irene Carruthers nee Rothery

I attended Arlecdon School, and I was lucky to have lived just around the corner on Parks Road so I did not have to travel far. I was five years old when I started school and my first teacher was either Miss Kelly or Miss Simpson. They both taught reception and infants. One of my best memories of early school was having our milk in the morning. In the winter, when it was very cold, the milk would freeze and lift the card board tops, which had a hole for your straw, right out of the bottle. The teacher would put the crate with the bottles up above the big stove to thaw the milk out. It was fun watching the tops, which had risen up due to freezing, pop down again. Later on, we were given Digestive Biscuits as well. I liked that very much.

The boys and girls played in separate playgrounds and had their own toilets too. I loved school dinners. At lunch time we all lined up in the corridor next to the kitchen area and Mrs Merrit and Mrs Vickers would serve us and then we would go to a class room that doubled up as a dining room to eat our meals. As we got older we had sewing lessons. I liked sewing but I didn't like knitting. Mrs Smith took us for sewing and knitting. We had visits from the school dentist and the 'nit nurse'. We had to go to Whitehaven Swimming Baths for swimming lessons.

Mr G. Walker was very strict and dealt out punishment where needed. One of the teachers I liked was Miss Kirkbride, she was very nice. Mr Jack Cook was a good teacher too. We also had a Mr Gedling and a Miss Adams. After the war, we had Mr C. Burns. He was strict. I had my very first telling off from him!

We had lovely Christmas parties. Our parents made the food. I remember my mother making the jellies in big dishes and fairy cakes. Altogether I enjoyed my school days even though we had to contend with the war being on. We all just carried on the best we could.

My family, Mam, Dad and brother, Joe, lived on Parks Road at Number 22. It was a 'two up and two down', a cold house with few facilities. We had no bathroom and had to use a tin bath in front of the living room fire. Water was heated in a boiler at the side of the living room range. The landlord had a tin sheeting hut built onto the back of the house which was supposed to be our back kitchen. There was a gas ring on a stone slab, a stone sink and that was all. The tap was inside but in the winter it would freeze. It was awful! Mam did most of the cooking in the living room on the range. She baked bread, cakes and teacakes. We shared two toilets with four houses and the wash house was shared as well. We all had different wash days. We had to light a fire under the 'set pot' to boil the water. We used dolly tubs to wash the clothes using a 'poss stick'. We also washed by hand using a small brush and Sunlight Soap. A mangle was used to remove the water and the clothes were then put out onto a line to dry.

We also had hens in one of the fields at the back of the house. They were a source of food when times were hard.

My Nanna Rothery lived at number 35 Parks Road and the doctor's surgery was held in her front parlour. Our doctors were Calder, Watson and Margaret Watson and for a while a lady doctor called Gatschalk.

Nanna was organist at the Methodist Chapel at Rowrah. She had an organ in the front room and my brother, mother and I would sing hymns and songs. Nanna could listen to the modern music on the radio and take it down in 'Tonic Solfa' so we did not have to spend money on sheet music.

My dad was called up into the army when I was 5 yrs old. I remember a letter coming and, after my Dad read it, Mam started to cry. I found out much later that no one in the family thought that Dad would be called up because he had had an accident working at Drigg and lost an eye, but he still had to go. We only saw him when he had leave.

Children had to entertain themselves. The boys played marbles and football on the Fairfield and there were swings, a slide and a seesaw. There was also what was called 'Giant Strides' to use. On this ride you would put your arm through the bar and run round as fast as you could and then launch yourself into the air. If there were a few of you it made it a much better ride. We had our sports days on the Fairfield. There were also tennis courts. I can remember girls skipping with long ropes across the road to see how many could skip together at one time.

The girls would dress up in their mother's clothes and use old net curtains for veils. We had our dolls prams too. We must have looked so funny in dad's hats and jackets parading down Parks Road, knocking on doors for pennies.

In the summer our mothers took us on picnics up to Kelton Head where we would pick hazel nuts to bring home. We would also go to Cogra Moss to pick bleaberries when they were ripe and by the time we got home we would be 'Blue Berries' – blue fingers and blue tongues! At Easter, mother would send us down to Willie Hodgson's lonning to pick young nettles, dandelions, Easterman Giants and sour docks to make herb pudding. She would soak pearl barley overnight and the next day boil spring cabbage and all the greens together. They were then drained and added to the barley with a big lump of butter. All the ingredients were then put into a tin dish and baked in the oven - it was fantastic!

Mrs McGuire, Cissie McGuire, Janie Ullock and Nanna Rothery outside 35 Parks Road

Irene with her brother Joe

My Nanna Rothery would give Joe and me our physic in the spring (Sulphur and Treacle). We never had spots or any tummy troubles after that. We were given Cod Liver Oil and Virol from the Clinic in Frizington, which was held in the Council Chambers. The nurse checked every thing that would keep us fit and well.

I would go with my Nanna to pick Burnets to make wine. In the autumn we would pick Rose Hips and make pocket money from them. The boys would go potato picking at the local farms. We, as children, would not be allowed to stray too far away from home because convoys of Prisoners of War used to come through our village, also army convoys.

I went to St. Michael's church with my mother and brother. It was a lovely walk in spring and in summer, but in the winter it was an ordeal. The Rev. Leycester Ward was the vicar. He was quite elderly, but very nice. We had a Sunday school at Arlecdon.

My brother and I were also honorary members of the Methodist Church. As Nanna, was the organist and a good Methodist, we were always included in the anniversaries. We had to stand up and recite from the Bible. We all sat on a stair-like platform. I didn't like climbing up there because I thought I would fall. I received my Lord Wharton prayer book for attendance at church and Sunday School.

When I was eleven, I was confirmed along with the other children who went to the Church of England. The girls were dressed in white and the boys wore little suits and ties. The Bishop of Carlisle came to confirm us and we had a tea party in the Sunday school afterwards.

It was about this time that a tragedy happened on Parks Road. Little Alan Towers was killed. He was sitting on the kerbside with some other boys when a large wagon passed and the suction dragged him under the wheels. He died instantly. It was the first time I had ever seen a dead person. All the children who wanted to were allowed to go to see him in his coffin. He looked like a little angel. I think it helped us to understand that he was not going to be here any more and was going to be with Jesus.

In 1944 Mrs Markham (a neighbour) called Joe and I to mother's bedroom to show us a tiny baby. He was in a big bottom drawer. I had heard a noise that night and thought it was Father Christmas, so for a while (I was only nine) I thought that he had brought the baby.

Two years later, my other brother was born so now we were in need of more room and that's why we moved to Frizington. It was wonderful to have an indoor toilet and bathroom and our own wash house and coal house.

Although I left Arlecdon when I was thirteen and a half to move to Frizington, I still have my roots in Arlecdon.

Patchwork and Poetry

In March 1949, the burial of Ann Dickinson, aged 91, of Kidburngill took place in Arlecdon churchyard. Ann was one of five daughters of John Dickinson and his wife, Margaret. They also had a son, John Key Dickinson who died in 1916 aged 63 years.

Ann had lived in the family home with her three unmarried sisters, caring for their father after the death of their mother, Margaret, in 1860, at the tragically young age of 38 years. One of her sisters, Mary, married Mr J.W. Mulcaster and was interred at Flimby in 1933 aged 82 years.

The four remaining sisters would possibly be the last of the Dickinsons to reside at Kidburngill, which, according to the memorial inscriptions in Arlecdon churchyard, had been the home of that particular branch of the family since the late 17th century.

*William Dickinson and his wife Jane
Photo courtesy of The Beacon*

A typical Cumbrian farming family, starting out as yeoman farmers, along with their neighbours and later, as they became more prosperous, they were described as 'gentleman' farmers. They married into other land owning families such as the Woods of Brownrigg, the Keys of Arlecdon Parks, the Flemings and Boadles of Wright Green and were not averse to lending each other money, charging interest on the loan - of course! One of the William Dickinsons was known as 'Banker Billy'. He issued his own bank notes, some of which can still be seen in Tullie House Museum.

Many of the sons followed other professions. One in particular was William Dickinson (1789-1882) who became a land surveyor, but was equally well known for his writings such as 'Cumbriana', various essays on agriculture, collections of Cumbrian dialect words and he composed poetry about local people and places. His dialect work about 'The Lamplugh Club' and the escapades of its members on the annual club day is very descriptive – and amusing.

Perhaps this artistic gene is carried on throughout the generations because in the early 19th century we find the Miss Dickinsons of Kidburngill producing beautiful patchwork quilts, one of which is now housed in the Fine Arts Collection at Tullie House Museum, where it was gifted by Mrs M. Hall in 1957. Another quilt by Ann Rawling, their next door neighbour at Wright Green Farm, was also gifted in1958 by Mr William Mulcaster, the husband of Mary, another sister who also wrote poetry. (See section on the rebuilding of the church 1900-1910)

Framed Diamond in the Square patchwork quilt by one of the Miss Dickinsons of Kidburngill, c. 1850. Photo courtesy of Tullie House Museum and Art Gallery.

Later, in the 20th century, two of the unmarried daughters, (Ann and Hannah), of John Dickinson were producing poetry.

According to E.R. Denwood in his *'Poets of Cockermouth and District'*, Annie (Ann), had started school at Arlecdon but later went to Miss Brindle's School at Greta Hall, Keswick, where she was taught in the school room which had once been the library of the poet, Robert Southey. It was there that she acquired her love of poetry and was soon contributing songs and poems to the columns of various local newspapers. In 1891 these were collected into a volume, *'Songs and Verses'*, printed for private circulation. She wrote about outdoor themes and her love of the hills, her animals and the changing seasons. In her poem, *'Lakeland'* she writes;

The city's din was left behind,
The rush and roar of men,
And sweet it was to find myself
In Lakeland once again.

In the second verse of *'The Old Black Mare'*, she expresses her love of horses and her joy of riding;

For often in the springtime,
At the closing of the day,
I would fling the saddle on her back,
And canter far away,
It mattered not how black was life
I left behind all care
When flying through the darkness
On the old black mare.

Annie was born in the middle of the 19th century just as the railway came to West Cumberland. Her father, along with the Boadle family of Wright Green, would no doubt receive a substantial sum of money from the railway company for the sale of his land to accommodate the railway line. Annie remained unimpressed by this modern form of transport as is obvious in this first verse of her poem, '*A Song of the Road*'

'Tis brave to mount at early dawn
When the coach to start is ready,
When nags are fresh, and harness bright,
And the coachman's hand is steady.
The whip goes whirling through the air,
The wheels spin gaily round,
And the horses' hoofs on the well- kept road
Give forth a gladsome sound.

Let those who like the railroad praise,
And boast the power of steam -;
Give me a seat by the coachman's side
Behind a well matched team.

Her sister, Hannah Dickinson, who died in1933, aged 77 years, also wrote verse, which appeared in local newspapers under the signature 'K'. Her poems dispense some good advice. For example, in the poem, '*Let It not Be You*', she entreats the reader, to withhold their temper, refrain from spreading scandal and finding fault with others as this extract demonstrates;

Some people to ill temper yield,
And afterwards they rue,
When they another's temper rouse,
But let not that be you.

Some readily will scandal spread
By tales half false, half true,
And damage others' characters,
But let it not be you.
And some are always finding fault
Whatever others do,
If wrong or right 'tis much the same,
But let not that be you.

She carries on in the same tone until in the final verse she advises the reader to be '*honest, capable and good*' and to '*sympathise with others' woes*'.

It is fascinating to consider these Dickinson daughters, sewing and writing to while away long winter evenings. Did they keep diaries in the same way as their father and his neighbours would have kept their farm journals? What changes they would have observed in farming practices and the development of the surrounding villages of Arlecdon and Asby as the mining industry brought in migrant workers from all over the British Isles. Perhaps, Kidburngill could have had its own version of the Bronte sisters? In any case, their work surely deserves to be promoted and recognised along with the efforts of other unsung poets in this quiet backwater of west Cumbria.

Health and Heroics!

In 1948 a National Health Service was introduced offering free health care at the point of need. Prior to this time all health treatment had to be paid for, usually by paying 4d or 6d a week to someone who collected door to door, to enable the resident to remain on the local 'doctor's list'.

Among the doctors who served in Arlecdon in those early years were Dr Haythornthwaite, Dr Colville, Dr Sharpe, Dr Calder and Dr Watson.

The doctor's surgeries were held in the front rooms of ordinary houses such as Gladys Gainford's at 32 Parks Road, the doctor's house on Rowrah Road and later in a house on Arlecdon Road.

Mrs Chorley, Tot's mother feeding her chickens

The local hospital was at Whitehaven, in the castle, a former home of the Lowther family. An isolation hospital for those suffering from tuberculosis was at Blencathra..

An orthopaedic children's hospital, the Ethel Hedley, was situated in a lovely spot on the shores of Lake Windermere. One Arlecdon lass, 'Tot' Chorley, spent a long time there as a patient. When she was finally discharged it was discovered that she had one foot larger than the other.

View from Tot's back garden.
Note the Reading Room on Fairfield

Fortunately, a good friend Bella, whom she had met in an Edinburgh Hospital, had the same problem but involving the opposite foot so for years whenever they got a new pair of shoes, they swapped – by post!!

Tot, who became Mrs Parker, lived on Arlecdon Road after she married. One day she heard a noise at her front door and when she went to look, there was Haggerty's bull making its way through the doorway into the house. This plucky little woman ran as best she could out of the back door shouting, "There's a bull in my lobby!" and raised the alarm. The school children were secured in the classrooms and everyone stayed indoors while Farmer Haggerty instructed his dogs to persuade the bull back into the nearby field, where it was occasionally allowed to graze.

Ernest Little and John Haggerty

1950 to 1959

The Coronation Carnival

Jennifer Carruthers

There was going to be a carnival in Arlecdon to celebrate the Queen's Coronation on 3rd July 1953. At school, all the names of the girls in the top class were put in a hat and drawn out to see who was to be the Carnival Queen. Margaret Nelson was the lucky girl to be pulled out first, so she was to be the Carnival Queen. Second out was Mary Carty, she was to be the Lady-in-Waiting. As Margaret lived on Arlecdon Parks Road, the attendants were selected from that row of houses. Derek Fitz Williams was the herald, Evelyn Witten, Lynn and Lorna Walker and Jennifer Arthur were the attendants. Keith Huddart and Joseph Lightfoot were the page boys.

So the children were chosen; it just left the mode of transport to be decided on. That was to be Jess, the cart -horse belonging to John Haggerty, the farmer on Arlecdon Parks Farm, pulling a wagon.

Jess and the wagon were both decorated with coloured crepe paper, which was cut in fringes and frills and twisted round the wooden frame to elaborate the farm wagon.

Coronation Carnival 1953

Father's milk horse, Mac, held by Uncle John Robert Vickers

Some former Carnival Queens...

Mary McQuire

Above: Kath Bowman nee Hodgson of Tilekiln Farm as Britannia in the 1930s and pictured right is Kath today

The day finally came. The children were loaded onto the Carnival Queen's float, and along with The Rose Queen, Brittania and others walking in fancy dress, the Carnival paraded round the village, finishing on the Fairfield. All the children were given a bag filled with a sandwich, an iced bun and a cake. Inevitably, the icing always stuck to the inside of the paper bag, so you had to bite it off. Photos were taken, prizes were presented and everyone had a good time.

I hope the real Queen had as an enjoyable time, riding in her golden coach, as we did riding on our farm wagon, with Jess brushed and combed with ribbons through her mane and tail, looking like she had never looked before.

Freda Jefferson

Electricity Comes to Arlecdon

In 1956 big changes came to the village. We were going to get electricity. House by house it was installed. People bought televisions and some, like Mrs Irving on Parks Road, invited the children of the village into their homes to watch 'Children's Hour'. The children queued up and down the street waiting to get in. They crowded in to the small living room, sitting two on every available seat and chair arm in the house. Those without seat stood, little ones sat on the floor at the front. We were asked to donate one penny to a charity box and enjoyed every minute. There was only BBC channel available at this time although one or two could watch ITV Granada if they could receive the signal from Caldbeck.

Good news! Mrs Stainton, who had the shop on Parks Road, now had electricity. That means she could have a freezer, and sell ice-cream and ice lollies. We children would not have to wait for the ice-cream vans to come around. We could have them when we liked - if we had the money!

Arlecdon Relatives

Yvonne Magridge (Stainton)

Once a week, in the late 1940s twin brother Bill, Dad and I walked to Arlecdon, to visit Gran Stainton, Uncle Bill, Auntie Cissie, cousins Alec and Gordon, armed with 'ration books' to get our weekly ration of sweets.

We travelled past the pond at the bottom end of Arlecdon, where Dad had fallen in age 3. He was rescued by being yanked out by his long blond curly locks. Everyone we passed said "How do Joe". All were in 'fine fettle' or 'fair to midlin'. Everyone in the world must know my Dad. A fact later confirmed, as in the 1930s depression, the only job going was as a steward on a ship bound for Canada. The crew were allowed ashore for a few hours before the return journey. As Dad descended the gang plank the first person he saw said "How do Joe". It was another lad from Arlecdon.

Uncle Bill and Auntie Cissie ran the sweet shop at number 10 where Bill and I carefully chose the sweets for our 2oz triangular bag, clutching them in our hot palms where they stuck together and to the sides of the bag. Dad had a bigger bag for the family to 'last the week'. One after dinner (in theory).

Cousin Gordon was about 2 years older and had red curly hair. Alex was 2 years older again with black wavy hair. I thought he was handsome. I remember having a ride on his back whilst Dad was refereeing the Arlecdon ladies football match - possibly versus Frizington. "How long will the game take?" I asked. "It depends" was the reply, "whenever it is reasonable to call a draw". The previous game had been played 90 minutes exactly and one team won. The losing team made life so unbearable for the next 12 months that survival tactics were needed. So my fair, honest Dad, a Methodist local preacher who really did practice what he preached, 'fixed the game'!

All the lads in Dad's family played football. Dad, Bill, Jack and Alec who had died at 19 had a trial for 'Workington Reds'. Stainton legs were noted on the football field, not for their beauty (I think they were a bit bandy) but their ability to pass and dribble a football.

Arlecdon Ladies Football Team 1950s. Back row L to R:- Gus Risman, Janie Adams, Mary Balance, Margaret Mc Creadie, Lilian Friers, Betty Huddart. Front row L to R: - L. Cass, Effie Hodgson, Lizzie Corlett, Margaret Cook (nee Irving), Jean Dixon, Amy Mason(nee Irving) – Was this the team Mr Stainton, the 'honest' referee, fixed the game for?

Gordon Stainton, Yvonne's cousin at St Michael's Church organ

"Aren't you proud that all your lads are playing for football teams?" Gran was asked. "No" said an unimpressed Gran. "It seems that all their brains are in their feet, I'd rather they had brains in their heads."

Whilst Uncle Bill, Auntie Cissie and the boys lived at No. 9, Gran and her brother Uncle Jim lived in No. 10. Uncle Jim was the star of the visit. He sat in a brown armchair between the fire range and the back room window behind the shop.

Uncle Jim had a 'peg leg' (apparently lost in a coal mining accident). The 'peg leg' was not just for helping him to get about but to keep naughty children in order. What a challenge! On annoying him as much as I dared he would unstrap the leather belt that went round his waist and over his shoulder, grasp the peg leg with both hands and wave it threateningly at the offender. I made a hasty retreat out of the back door into the yard and stayed until I thought things might calm down, (trying not to be so annoying on cold wet days). I loved Uncle Jim; he was the most interesting person I'd ever met.

Christmas in the Early 1950s

Jennifer Carruthers

Christmas was on the way, just a couple of weeks to go; we were getting excited, looking forward to the school party. Everyone was asked to contribute food such as jellies, sandwiches and cakes. Games were played like 'Farmers in the Den' 'Pass the Parcel' 'Musical Chairs,' and I remember trying to eat a block of chocolate wearing hat scarf and huge gloves, using a knife and fork, in limited time.

We wrote notes to Father Christmas, telling him what we would like for presents. These were posted up the chimney. Father Christmas had his fairies up the chimney listening to hear if we were well behaved.

We were taken to meet Father Christmas at the Beehive Department Store at Whitehaven, where he came each year. He had his own grotto in the basement near the toy department. We told Father Christmas what we would like for Christmas, usually feeling very nervous of this strangely dressed old man, whereupon he would gave us a present

There was also an animated laughing man. You put a penny in the slot and he set off laughing, and rocking about. This relieved the tension of the visit as some children were crying with fear of this stranger; others were trying to be brave.

We had a real Christmas tree bought from Ronnie Place, a Frizington greengrocer who also had a mobile shop. He called each week and we children bought a '3d bag'. This was a brown paper bag of fruit usually an apple, an orange, a few cherries or monkey nuts, what ever was in season. The tree went up and we were allowed to help to decorate it with things saved from previous years that had been carefully wrapped and stored safely. The fairy went on the top, and as there was no electricity in the village a large battery was used to power the coloured lights. Silver tinsel, which had been wrapped in dark blue paper to stop it from tarnishing, was draped round the finished tree.

Mistletoe was hung in the lobby as you came through the front door, and holly was placed behind pictures hanging on the walls and on top of the wall clock. One piece of holly was always left in place until Shrove Tuesday when it was taken down and burned on the fire (I think you were supposed to fry your pancakes with it to ward off evil spirits!). Paper decorations were hung from the corners of the room to the centre of the ceiling, and looped round the room with balloons tied between the loops, this was all done after we were in bed and there was much excitement when we came down in the morning.

On Christmas Eve we hung up our stockings, borrowed from our Granddad as he had the longest stockings (hand knitted by Grandma). We also had a pillowcase, for the bigger things. Both stockings and pillowcases were left at the bottom of the bed.

Christmas morning, we wakened early when it was still dark. There was no electricity so we couldn't just switch on the lights to see if Father Christmas had been, "Has he been?", we asked each other excitedly. We would scrabble to the bottom of the bed and feel around for the parcels and shout with excitement, "He's been", thus waking the rest of the household. They didn't seem as excited as us, and we were told to be quiet and go back to bed and sleep as it was too early to be up.

The stocking was filled with little things, like pencils and rubbers. Always a tangerine wrapped in silver paper, a sugar mouse, a bag of chocolate money and nuts. Also, a 3d piece minted in that particular year was found at the very bottom. We got one main present, such as a doll's cot, and in the pillow case were jig-saw puzzles, an annual, crayons and a colouring book, a selection box, always a new knitted out-fit for one of my dolls. Later I would find the doll down stairs, having had its face and possibly the rest of it washed, looking like new and ready for its new clothes.

The morning was spent playing with the toys and dinner was at noon. We would have turkey or sometimes goose. My sister remembers coming home on the bus from Whitehaven with Mam on Christmas Eve. She had bought a goose at Dewhursts, the butchers, and the head and neck were poking out of the top of the shopping bag. (You didn't get them frozen and in plastic bags in those days.) There were always eight or nine for dinner including grandparents and an aunt and uncle. The turkey would be carved and Mam would ask who wanted a leg.. The grown ups seemed to liked legs, so we all would shout out that we wanted a leg and Mam would laugh and say, "It's not a spider you know it's a turkey with only two legs". This was followed by plum pudding and rum sauce. We pulled crackers and wore paper hats.

After the pudding was cleared, a table decoration in the shape of a swan was brought to the table. It was made of cardboard and covered in cotton wool. The back of the swan was hollow and there were small gifts inside. Picking a numbered string, hanging outside the body of the swan, was how the gifts were chosen. We were just as excited about these small gifts, as the rest of the presents received that day, and, being siblings, often fratched because somebody got something you wanted, so bargains and swaps had to be made.

The rest of the day was spent playing and I suspect we went to bed early as we had been wakened since early morning.

Eskett

There's only Eskett Quarry remaining now, but in the late 19th & 20th Centuries, Eskett was a small hamlet with a close-knit community. It was situated about 2 miles off the B5086 between Frizington and Arlecdon and about 8 miles from Whitehaven.

It is classed as in the parish of Lamplugh and years ago it had been in the demesne of Eskatt & Salter, the main landowner being a Mrs Margaret Dickinson. It comprised of a row of cottages called Fair View, built next to Ennerdale Hall, or Eskett Mansion as most people know it, two more modern detached houses, then down the road past the quarry there were three farmsteads – Eskett Farm, Eskett Farm and Eskett Parks Farm.

ENNERDALE HALL

Surprisingly, little is known about Ennerdale Hall, considering it was quite a large, imposing, Victorian building. It has been described as 'rambling and rather ugly', built of mustard yellow brick and sandstone, with tall chimney stacks. We don't know exactly when it was built, but it was there when the 1881 Census was conducted. John Postlethwaite , the land and mine owner, lived there with servants and a Sarah Mossop was his housekeeper. She went on to become Mrs Postlethwaite in 1882.

The hall was built by the builder, Charles Pearson. What has proved rather misleading in my research, is that it appears that it wasn't originally called Ennerdale Hall, but Fair View, which, to my mind, is a more apt name for it. Ennerdale Hall implies its situation as Ennerdale, but is, in fact, about two miles from Ennerdale, though I daresay it probably had a nice view over towards Ennerdale.

Although it had extensive grounds, it doesn't look as though these were fully developed till the new owner took over after Postlethwaite's death. This was George J. Snelus, who, as well

Ennerdale Hall

as giving the place a new identity, was responsible for the development and the layout of the grounds and gardens. He incorporated greenhouses next to the Fair View Cottages, as they were called at the time, and he brought home all kinds of species of flowers from his foreign travels, in particular orchids, which he built up into a considerable collection. These were housed in the very greenhouses where I have some vivid childhood memories.

JOHN POSTLETHWAITE

He lived from 1842 to 1886, the son of John and Isabella Postlethwaite from Whitehaven, and was the first owner of Ennerdale Hall. His father was a solicitor and public notary, operating from 14 Scotch Street in Whitehaven, but at some point must have spent some time in Melbourne, Australia, as that is where John was born. John later became a solicitor and had his office at 12 Scotch Street, Whitehaven. The Mossop family also lived at that address as Mrs Mossop was the 'keeper of the office' as well as housekeeper. They had a daughter, Sarah, who later became Mrs Postlethwaite although a lot younger than her husband. They were married in March 1882 when she was 22 yrs and he was 40.

At some point, circa 1881, John Postlethwaite moved to Fair View, Eskett, as he was now the owner of Eskett Iron Ore Mine and the surrounding land. The 1881 census shows Sarah and her father living with him and Sarah was the housekeeper.

The marriage didn't last long, as Sarah died in April 1884, age 23 yrs, in Christchurch, Hampshire, and was buried in Arlecdon churchyard. Did she die in childbirth? There doesn't appear to be a record of birth or death. However, it wasn't long before John followed her, as he died with congestion of the lungs, on 24th June 1886, aged 44 years. In his will, he left the builder, Charles Pearson, a silver trowel.

During his short life, he had achieved quite a lot. As well as being a solicitor and owner of Postlethwaite's Eskett Mining Co, Eskett, he owned another iron ore pit at Moor Row. Obviously a learned man, he had quite a lot of letters behind his name. Apparently, latterly, he was heavily in debt, probably due to the failing of his mine, an unsuccessful lawsuit against another mining company for this failure, plus investment put into building Fair View, as it was a large building. It is believed that he sold it for £2,000 and this would be to Mr Snelus, who appears to have re-named it Ennerdale Hall.

GEORGE J. SNELUS

He was Postlethwaite's successor at Ennerdale Hall. He lived there before 1891 (exact date of moving in, not known), with his wife, Lavinia, and family, until his death in June 1906. He was born in Camden Town, London, in 1837 and when he was fourteen, he was a pupil teacher.

His adult career wasn't in teaching, however, - he went to university and studied engineering, becoming an eminent metallurgist and expert on iron ore. It is reckoned that he invented the Bessemer process of iron making although it was credited to Mr Bessemer! He travelled all over the world giving lectures, as well as writing papers on iron ore, which were translated into many languages. When he was at Ennerdale Hall, he was the manager of Workington Iron and Steel Works. The family lived a grand life at the hall, having quite a number of servants. Many well-connected people visited the hall in horse-drawn carriages for social occasions, afternoon tea etc.

The Eventful Wedding Day of Miss Snelus

Arlecdon has seen the effects of severe weather over the years but the 'Big Freeze' of 1895 disrupted not only the everyday life of the villagers but a very special day for Miss Mabel Eliza Snelus of Ennerdale Hall. February 6th that year was to be her wedding day.

She and her family and friends arrived at the church by two o'clock but the bridegroom unfortunately did not!

They waited until three o'clock and when the bridegroom still had not appeared they set off to return to Ennerdale Hall only to find that the roads were impassable because of the heavy snowfall.

They had no alternative but to remain in the church overnight.

St Michael's Church after the snowstorm. From 'A History of Arlecdon and Frizington' by the Rev. E. H. Sugden

Memorial stone of Mabel Howes

It would appear that the groom, Mr John Groome Howes and his best man had attempted to reach the church on foot from Havercroft, Lamplugh, but were forced to return home by the severe snowstorm, not realising that the bride was waiting at the church.

The next morning the bride's brother and another guest set out from the church and after a great deal of effort, crawling through snowdrifts and ditches, reached Havercroft some five miles away and managed to lead the groom and best man back to the church where the wedding took place.

The honeymoon in London was postponed and the bride and groom and their guests celebrated at Ennerdale Hall by dancing the night away.

Some guests including the Rev A.F. Curwen of Harrington tried to return home by rail from Winder Station but the train became stuck in the snow and so they ended up spending another night away from home, this time in the stationmaster's house. They sat around a fire which was kept burning all night with coal from the locomotive.

This story has a sad ending. Mrs Howes gave birth to a baby girl on December 12th 1895 but became very ill with fever and despite the efforts of a number of doctors she died at Havercroft on January 11th 1896, eleven months after her eventful wedding day.

Her tombstone is one of the more ornate in the churchyard and is next to that of her father.

Interestingly, the bridegroom, John James Groome Howes was born in Melbourne, Australia. His father was William Howes described as a gentleman. John and his two brothers, Henry and Philip, sailed to England in 1880 and attended Highbury House Boarding School for Boys in Hastings. On leaving school he took up a career as a mining engineer. Our research leads us to believe that he remarried in Cockermouth in 1898 and travelled to Australia in 1907 with his wife and four year old daughter.

It would appear that the daughter born to Mabel Howes, shortly before her death, survived and it is believed that she may have gone to Canada.

THE WRIGHT FAMILY

They lived at Ennerdale Hall immediately after Snelus, until John Wright, the father, died in 1926. His wife Margaret Jane, then bought the Central Hotel in Whitehaven. John had originated from Southport and was a ship's blacksmith. While at sea, he was injured in a storm and lost his leg, so he made a false leg for himself.

Before coming to the hall, he lived at Yeathouse Road, Frizington, where he was a grocer. He and Margaret Jane had seven children – Alfred (born 1891) who went to America; Ethel (b. 1893) who married Thomas Ireland and lived locally; John (b. 1895) who was killed in the army; Maggie (b. 1898) who lived at Cleator Moor; Iona (b.1901) who married Johnny Birney and had a shop in Frizington; Olga (b.1903) who moved away to Wales, and Monica (b.1911) who also moved away.

By all accounts, Iona was a very attractive young woman with a personality to match. She and Olga were very musical and entered the local Music Festivals. They also organised concert parties at the hall as well as Garden Fetes.

THE SHEPHERD FAMILY

The Shepherds lived at Ennerdale Hall from about 1928 to the mid 1950s. Initially there were the parents, three sons and one daughter. One son went to be a priest in Canada, another, Arthur would now be in his nineties, if still alive. He went to Arlecdon School with Tom Slater, who still lives at Winder Brow, and went into the R.A.F.. Gordon, the youngest was killed. Florrie, the daughter, is the one that people remember best. She used to have a sweet shop in part of the mansion, and children from all over, went there to get their sweets. You didn't go into the shop – Florrie served you through an open window. Her father had a 'fruit and veg' round, going all round the local area with his horse and cart.

The family seemed to have been very enterprising. It was during this time that Mr Shepherd applied for two houses to be built where the Hall stables had been. These houses were called Hillcrest and Hazel Mount. For a while between 1932 and 1944, part of the mansion was used as a Youth Hostel. It opened from Easter to the end of September every year and was classed as 'a country-house, a relic of the lost iron-mining industry'. It wasn't a particularly popular Youth Hostel, as it wasn't in a good situation, i.e. not near to the mountains and lakes and Ennerdale was over two miles away. Consequently, it closed in 1944. During the war, the Shepherds had evacuees from Newcastle, but they didn't stay long, as it was too remote for them – it was too far away from the fish'n chip shops and pubs!

Another popular memory of older members of our community is of the mansion during the 'Shepherd era', when members of the public went to play tennis on the courts which had been built by the previous occupants. Locals would go and play tennis, then have a picnic in the grounds. On Saturday nights, there was usually a dance in the big hall and Mr Shepherd would play the concertina. Afternoon teas were also provided.

In 1956/7 Florrie and her father left the mansion for pastures new – I believe they went to run a Guest House in Blackpool.

CHILDHOOD MEMORIES OF ESKETT

Here I am circa 1953/4, on the steps of 4 Fair View, Eskett, with my sister Kathleen. I was 6 and she was 3. I can vividly remember the flecked tweed coat and the Fair-Isle beret I was wearing!

Fair View consisted of four terraced houses, built prior to the census of 1881, No. 2 being a double-fronted one, and ours was the end one adjoining the boundary wall of the mansion (as we called it).

An Irish family called O'Gorman lived at No. 1. There was mother & father, John and Margaret, with children Patrick, Mary and Christine. No. 2, was occupied by Tom Bowness, an ageing bachelor – he lived on

Kathleen and Jean Mason at 4 Fair View circa 1950s

his own after his sister married and moved to Windergate. She was now Mrs Bailiff and was a Piano Teacher.

I actually went to her for piano lessons every Saturday morning and thought nothing, at age 9, of walking alone from Eskett to Windergate via Bobby Wilson's Winder Farm. You just wouldn't do this now! Jack and Grace Litt lived at No. 3 and they were good neighbours. Mrs Litt was a 'real lady' and was sister to the Nicholson brothers who farmed at Eskett.

They had an only son, John, who was in the R.A.F.. The Litts were the first on the row to have television and I can remember sometimes going into their house to watch it, especially Phil Silvers in the Sergeant Bilko Show and the Queen's Coronation. We lived at No. 4 and my father was a fitter at the quarry until he left and went to work at Sellafield in the early 1950s.

Fair View, built circa 1881, was aptly named, as from the long front gardens, you had a lovely panoramic view of the countryside from Waterloo Terrace, right over Frizington and onto parts of Cleator and Cleator Moor. Next to No. 1 was the 'drying green', a fenced grassy area, which was used by the O'Gormans and no-one else. Beside that were two more modern houses, namely Hillcrest and Hazel Mount. These were built circa 1934, where part of the mansion stables were. Then, along from them, in a triangular shape, edged by a high wall, were the disused kennels.

Some Eskett Residents. L to R: - Mary and Christine O'Gorman, Margaret O'Gorman and Jack Litt, Patrick O'Gorman and Tom Bowness

Fair View Houses

We didn't know, as children, anything about them apart from 'you never got to go in' - it was all rather secretive. In Hillcrest lived the Teare family, Bill and Edith, with their children John, Audrey and David. Bill was a teacher at St. Paul's School, Frizington. A couple called Mr and Mrs Hellam, occupied Hazel Mount, but I can't really remember anything about them, except that they were elderly and we didn't see them often. The kennels had originally been the stables for Ennerdale Hall. Although these were defunct when I lived at Eskett, they had been used as kennels for greyhounds by Tom Bowness, who lived in the big house on Fair View. He bred these dogs for a Mr Kerr, in Whitehaven.

We children were never stuck for playing ideas at Eskett, as we were all much of an age and we had some wonderful times – it was a child's paradise. My most vivid memories are of playing in the mansion grounds before and after the mansion was demolished.

We never ventured into the mansion itself, which was then in a derelict state, probably because parents had told us never to go in it – and in those days you always did what your parents told you! I remember well, when the mansion was demolished.

We Fair View children, about half a dozen of us, would stand on the railway bank, well out of harm's way, absolutely mesmerized watching this gigantic machine 'to-ing and fro-ing' on its tracks. It was a huge green crane with red trim, belonging to Greggains of Maryport, with a hoist and large chains holding a big boulder. The crane would swing round and the momentum of the boulder would go smashing against the outside walls of the building and they would collapse.

One day, our fascination turned to horror when external walls, internal walls AND floors came crashing down. There was so much noise, dust and debris, but there was also a sense of panic. One of the labourers had been standing on the top floor and had come hurtling down with everything else – that obviously was not supposed to happen! He was rescued from the rubble by other workers and brought into our house to wait for a doctor or an ambulance. Fortunately, he wasn't badly injured, more shocked than anything, but looked quite a sight to a young child – all dirty, dishevelled and with the odd graze. What, I think, made it appear more gruesome to me, was that he had quite a severe hare lip and I'd never seen anything like that before. He was given a drink – I don't know if it was tea or something stronger, and not long after, an ambulance came and took him to hospital to be checked over. As far as I was aware, he was fine.

Another vivid memory was playing where the numerous greenhouses were. These had been brick structures at the base with wooden glazed frames at the top. Only the base walls remained and within these, we played at houses, schools etc. as the low walls were ideal for having different rooms.

I remember on many an occasion, playing with old kitchen utensils, cutlery, buckets etc. and making mud pies for our 'make-believe' food. Also, I remember playing at schools, when I was always the teacher and poor John Teare got his sums wrong, I hit him over the head with a frying pan! If John Teare ever reads this, I hope he will forgive me!!!!!

The mansion grounds also provided us with great places to hide, so Hide'n Seek was one of our favourite games and because the possibilities of hidey places were so huge, we were often not found and search parties were often sent to seek us! We also had tree houses up some of the larger trees. We would also pick primroses and snowdrops which grew profusely in the gardens.

The area round the mansion was idyllic before the quarry expanded too much. I can remember roaming the surrounding fields looking for wild strawberries, 'dathering grass', vetch, marguerites and wild orchids. However, we knew to keep out of the fields at hay-time, something we watched, with great interest, every summer. We also used to get enjoyment from watching the steam trains travelling past the back of our houses, going from Eskett Quarry to Rowrah Quarry and elsewhere. There was the sound of the train, the smoke and the cheery wave of the engine driver, one Reg Higgins.

Train journeys dwindled as more lorries were used to lead stone from the quarry. My dad worked there as a fitter, so we children knew most of the quarry lorry drivers, and it was with them, I often got a lift in their wagons to Arlecdon School. Nothing was thought of this at the time, but you wouldn't be able to do this nowadays. It saved me walking 2-3 miles to school and probably saved me many a wetting. It was with this in mind that I recently talked to present Arlecdon schoolchildren about how they travel to school. I will write about this later.

In 1958, I passed my 11+ and went to the Grammar School at Whitehaven. We moved to the top of Skelsceugh Road, Winder, to be nearer the bus route. I often think back to my early childhood days and what a wonderful environment to be brought up in, but was glad that we moved when I was ten. To a teenager, wanting to see more of the world and venturing out more independently, Eskett was too remote a place to live!

THE ESKETT FARMS

Beyond the mansion and the quarry, on the road to Salter one way and Redbeck, the other were three farms. Two were called Eskett Farm and the other was Eskett Parks Farm.

When I was little they were farmed by the Nicholson brothers, the Gaskell family and the Jacksons, although there had been various other tenants/owners over the years. Gaskells had been there since the late 1800s and Nicholsons since the early 1900s. Jacksons only came to Eskett Parks Farm in the 1950s – it was earlier farmed by the Dixons and then the Stephensons. The family living at Eskett Farm prior to the Nicholsons, was the Whinn family, which leads us on nicely to the next section.

The Whinn Family of Eskett Farm

Eskett Farm was one of three in the small community of Eskett. At one time a family called Whinn lived there. The head of the household in the 1891 census was a Mary Whinn, widow of Samuel Whinn, who had died sometime during the previous decade. Mary had a son, Samuel and two daughters, Jane, born 1868 and Hannah Mary, born 1873. Both were christened at Arlecdon church.. The girls were obviously trained in the sewing skills required by young ladies of the time. (See samplers)

Hannah Mary appears to have died young and by October 1897 Jane is living at The Result, Frizington with her mother and is about to marry William Suddart of Haile.

It is interesting to note the details of the wedding in the newspaper reports at that time, which included descriptions of the fashions of the day such as 'the satin straw hat trimmed with ostrich tips, satin ribbon and orange blossom' and the fact that the groom, who had just returned from working in South Africa, gave his bride the gift of a diamond brooch. It is also intriguing that no other members of the Whinn family attended the wedding and that Jane was given away by the Rev. P. N. Kennedy, vicar of Wythop. Where was brother Samuel at this time?

In the 1901 census the family was living at Winder Gate with Mary Whinn, still head of the household with William Suddart, her son-in-law, described as an Assurance Agent and Jane and her daughter Hannah Mary, known as Mamie, born 1899.

They appeared fairly well to do as William drove a Rexette car (AO 585) registered in November 1907 and Mamie appears as a beautiful curly haired toddler in 'Cousin Charley's Magazine' Vol. III, No.1, in 1901. She could easily have been the 'Miss Pears' of her day! The magazine, which ran from

Sampler by Hannah Mary Whinn aged 10. Arlecdon 1883

Sampler by Jane Whinn aged 11 years. Arlecdon 1879

1899 to 1901, was described as 'A Journal for Little Folks about Little Folks' and was published and printed by Brash Brothers Ltd of Cockermouth.

It featured stories and competitions and encouraged contributions from the readership.*

Mamie married Thomas George Jones, the son of a Frizington miner, who, incidentally, had had also worked in South Africa. How they met is not known and a puzzling postcard, depicting two lovers, suggests that at one time Thomas had to employ a little subterfuge in his courtship of Mamie.

The post card, dated 1915 is addressed to Grace Nicholson at Eskett Farm but the message is to Mamie and reads,

'*Dear Mamie,*

Just a line hoping you are quite well. Have been expecting a letter all day. Hope you received the small parcel etc.

Love from

(Initials -probably Thomas George Jones)'

Jane, William and Mamie Suddart circa 1908.

Was Grace employed as a go-between? She remained a good friend of the family and married a Jack Litt who worked at Eskett Quarry. At one time they lived at Fern Knoll, Waterloo Terrace where William Jones, the son of Mamie and Thomas, remembers visiting on a number of occasions. He particularly recalls being shown up to the large attic which he was told was used for cock-fighting! Grace and Jack later lived at Fair View cottages, Eskett.

An article about the magazine appeared in the Cumbria Family History Society's magazine in November 2005 written by William Jones, the son of Mamie, to whom the authors are grateful for the information and photographs for this piece.

ESKETT TODAY

Only memories and the quarry now remain. As the quarry has extended over the years, it has bought up all the surrounding land, Ennerdale Hall being demolished in the fifties, with Fair View houses, Hillcrest and Hazel Mount being demolished in the nineties. The gardens of the hall still remain, but are very run-down and wild, but are still bordered on one side by the original boundary wall. What used to be the drive up to the mansion is now the sweeping bend in the road leading up to the quarry. Fair View is now just a grassed-over area, so this article, hopefully, will serve as a reminder that at one time, this small area of Eskett was quite vibrant!

ARLECDON SCHOOL SURVEY (mentioned earlier)

It had always been the tradition that Eskett children attended Arlecdon School, although Eskett was in Lamplugh parish. Arlecdon was about two miles away, so it was a fair hike to school and back. Even in the 1950s, like many families, we didn't have a car, so it was Shanks's Pony or a lift in a quarry lorry. This was quite acceptable then, but provoked the thought that you wouldn't dare do it nowadays.

Other pupils attending Arlecdon School then, came from the immediate surrounding area of Arlecdon, Rowrah, Asby, Winder and Waterloo Terrace. It was decided to look at where today's Arlecdon pupils came from and how they get to school. Findings were quite surprising. Of the Juniors surveyed, not many lived in the village, although the school is portrayed as a village school.

Out of 17 surveyed, 5 were from Arlecdon, 4 from Rowrah, 2 from Asby, 1 from Winder, 1 from Cleator Moor, 1 from Cleator, 1 from Moresby Parks, 1 from Frizington and 1 from as far away as Workington. So there was quite a proportion of pupils from outside the catchment area. Obviously with being spread out far and wide, the method of getting to school is different, with the bulk of children now coming in parents' cars, even the very local children – only a handful walked!

Some other interesting information...

Did anyone know that once over, Waterloo Terrace was called Glebe Cottages and Fernknoll was called Waterloo Villa?

In the 1881 Census, Waterloo Villa and Glebe Cottages (9 of them) were recorded.

The 1891 Census recorded Waterloo Villa and Waterloo Terrace, as did the 1901 Census.

Yet, Fernknoll, as we know it, has above its front door in the original stone, the name Fernknoll and the date of 1877. Very interesting!!!

And why Waterloo, I wonder? .....The Battle of Waterloo was 1815, long before the houses were built.

Perhaps someone might be able to shed some light on this!

Young farmers in the 1950s

Evelyn and Robin Ackerley whose family farmed Brownrigg for over 30 years from 1949 (Note the milk churns and the rather large boots!). Brownrigg is synonymous with the Wood family who lived there for many generations from the early 18th century, marrying into most of the local landowning/yeoman farming families of the era such as the Jacksons, Mossops, Sumptons and Dickinsons.

Below: Brownrigg curve with farm in background circa 1930. By kind permission of the Cumbrian Railways Association

1960 to 1969

Best Foot Forward

Cloggers and shoemakers or cordwainers were once important and respected members of rural, mining and industrial communities. Historical evidence suggests that clogs may have been worn as early as in the 16th century, when people would wear pattens or wooden soles which were strapped directly onto the feet or onto early leather shoes to protect them when walking and working outside. There appears to have been a long tradition of clog and shoe making in Arlecdon going back as far as the mid 19th century.

In Sugden's *'History of Arlecdon and Frizington' (1897),* it is recorded that the following families had businesses in the village:-

1829 Moses Stainton Asby – shoemaker

1829 JohnSumpton Arlecdon – shoemaker

1847 Moses Stainton Asby – shoemaker

1847 Jacob Sumpton – clogger

1847 Thomas Bailiff ,Moss Gill – shoemaker

1880 Jonathan Branthwaite – shoemaker/clogger

1883 James Hannah – shoemaker

1883 Issac Mossop – shoemaker (Asby)

1901 Jonathan Branthwaite – boot/shoemaker

1906 James Carruthers – clogger

Photos by Ian Stockdale. Courtesy of The Beacon, Whitehaven

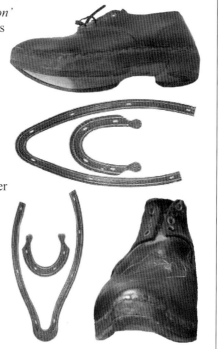

The last clogger/shoe repairer in Arlecdon was Thomas Balance who carried on the trade from the 1930s to the 1960s.

Traditionally, the basic clog consists of wooden soles and leather uppers. Although most types of wood have been used to make the soles, the favourite woods are Alder and Sycamore. Clog irons or caulkers are nailed onto the base of the sole at the front and heel. These provide good grip and stop the wood wearing out. The leather upper is treated with wax and oil, which makes it almost totally waterproof. A well-made pair of clogs could last for up to 20 years.

School children circa 1900

Clogs became symbolic of the industrial North, but they were actually worn all over the country. They were at their most popular during the late 19th Century, during the industrial revolution. Workers on farms and in quarries, iron ore mines, mills and factories needed strong, cheap, durable footwear that could be easily repaired.

Clogs have therefore long had an association with industry and manual labour, and gave rise to the idea that clogs were only for the working class and the poor, rather than the 'well off', as the middle and upper classes tended to aspire to wearing 'proper' shoes or boots.

As the 19th century drew to a close and the 20th century began, clogs rapidly became less popular and because they were seen by many as the footwear of the poor, a stigma developed around the wearing of them.

With the advent of WW2, clogs experienced a renaissance in popularity. Leather was in short supply and ration coupons were needed to buy leather-soled shoes and boots. The materials for clogs were more readily available and they proved to be durable and easier to repair than others types of footwear.

Clog boots were particularly popular with farmers and road workers, as the wooden sole kept them out of mud and insulated their feet from the heat, cold and damp. It became commonplace to see children wearing clogs for school.

Irene Carruthers (nee Rothery) remembers paying regular visits to the last clogger in Arlecdon, namely Thomas (Tommy) Balance, in the 1930s.

"I'd run up from Parks Road with the clogs, continue up Arlecdon Road and turn in at the Sunday School and then up back lonning that ran behind Mona Street to Tommy Balance's hut. When you went in, the first thing you noticed was the smell of leather and wood. As you looked around it was like an Aladdin's cave of machinery, wood, knives, the

big belt for polishing and the caulkers were hanging in big bundles from the ceiling with the little heel caulkers in boxes for all the different sizes. The uppers were stacked according to colours and size. The most memorable thing for me as a little child was waiting for the job to be finished, as I was always entertained by the many pictures of canaries and budgerigars all around the hut - Tommy was an avid 'birdman'. You could hear his own birds twittering in the huts nearby while you waited. I found that the clogs were hard and uncomfortable unless you had really good thick wool socks. In the winter, it was always fun to see who could get the highest pad of snow on the bottom, and who would end up with the cockled ankles. They also doubled up as great ice skates too! They were great because your feet were never cold as the clog raised you up off the ground and the wood kept your feet bone dry. My brothers wore the high ankled ones with the laces and my favorite ones were red with a strap and button fastening - but the older girls preferred the clasp fasteners. Later on, we started to wear clogs with rubber instead of iron caulkers, they were quieter, less slippy, but sadly they didn't make the sparks fly!"

Irene is the great great granddaughter of Jonathan Branthwaite (1883) who was a clogger/shoemaker working from 50 Parks Road, Arlecdon. Coincidentally, her husband, Chris, is also descended from a local clog making family.

Since the late 1950s there has been a steady decline in demand for clogs. Where you would have had at least one clog maker in most villages in England and Scotland in the early 1900s, there are today only a few in the whole of the UK.

Jonathan Branthwaite

Connie wearing Granny's clogs

Kart Racing at Kelton Head

Joseph Edgar, Iredale's father started at Lamplugh as an Agricultural Engineer, building farm machinery by hand. Anything a farmer wanted, he built. Nothing was impossible to him and work was his only interest. The word 'pleasure' was not in his vocabulary.

He acquired land at Rowrah, purchased an ex army Nissen hut from Cockermouth and dismantled it and erected it on the site at Rowrah. As times changed the business evolved into the modern car dealership it is to day

After Joseph retired, Iredale took over the business. Terry was then the apprentice and, as a hobby, built a Go Kart. He started racing on the old airfield at Haverigg and became very successful.

One Sunday, his grandfather, curious to know what Terry was doing, travelled to Haverigg and seeing how successful he was, offered to help repair and improve the performance of his kart, using his past skills as an engineer.

Terry Edgar with grandfather Joseph

The last two years of Joseph's life proved to be the most enjoyable, having at last learnt the art of relaxation, through his interest in his grandson's karting activities.

As a result, Iredale Edgar and Partners recognised the potential of Kelton Head quarry as a Kart Track and took in hand its conversion. 1963 saw the opening of the track.

Over the years it has become a noted venue for initiating the careers of many of today's Formula One racing drivers, including David Coulthard, Allan McNish, Jenson Button, Lewis Hamilton and will, hopefully, produce many more in the future.

Rowrah Co-op

The Cleator Moor Cooperative Society was formed in 1858, one of the first to follow in the footsteps of the 'Rochdale Pioneers'.

By 1878 they had established thirteen branches, one of which was at Rowrah and it soon became a very busy establishment and meeting place for the local populace.

Connie Irving, daughter of Henry Thompson, Co-op manager in the 1930s, recalls:

> *"Who could forget the Co-op building where all the food was weighed and packed in little parcels by hand, even the pepper had to be weighed and wrapped up. At the back of the main shop was a building called the flour room. A young boy was always employed in it before moving to work in the main store. People from Arlecdon, Asby, Kirkland, Lamplugh and Winder used to come with wooden bogies and old prams to carry the flour, hen food etc, home.*

Rowrah Co-op circa 1900. Photo courtesy H. Hicks

Once a week one of the employees had to cycle to outlying villages to collect grocery orders and a Mr Joe Thompson from the farm at Pasture Road, used to bring a horse and cart and deliver the goods. (An early Tesco on line!)

Farmers from as far away as Loweswater used to come with butter and fresh eggs, which were collected at Rowrah Co-op and taken to the warehouse at Cleator Moor to be distributed to other branches.

Of course, there was the Drapery Department next door with Mrs Laura Edmonds in charge. She sold curtains, dress material, clothing, shoes, wool etc – everything the busy housewife needed".

Val Fell remembers working at Rowrah Co-op at the beginning of 1966:-

"There were three of us working at the shop, Mr Rule, the manager, Eleanor Campbell and myself. Mr Rule was also the manager of the drapery department next door. The drapery assistant, Ann, married Mr Rule and therefore, because of the rules that existed at that time, had to leave. Married women were not employed by the Cleator Moor Co-operative Society.

There were a number of large metal containers in the storeroom, which were fed via hoppers from above. You had to be very careful that you put the correct item in its specific hopper, e.g. grit, hen food, maize, flour, otherwise it could cause great confusion! There were few pre packed goods. Most things had to be weighed out by the shop assistants."

There was also a mobile shop that had to be restocked weekly.

Shop assistant, Annie Kirby, helped to deliver goods to outlying farms and villages.

When the store closed at Easter in 1966, the staff members were employed in other Co-op stores.

Annie Kirby, later Annie Kirkbride, with Eleanor Campbell on her right, who later went to work in Rowrah Co-op, Kathleen Campbell and David McKenzie

L to R:- Tom Gaffney (Head Counterman) and Ted Blacklock (Manager) 1950s

1970 to 1979

Arlecdon Junior Rugby Club

For generations, Arlecdon had always had a footballing tradition until May 1977, when Arlecdon Junior Rugby Club was founded by Raymond Burns and Tom Crewdson. The teams played on the Fairfield and they used the Sunday School as change-rooms – complete with tin baths! Tom's family washed the strips, made soup for after the matches and cleaned up after the boys! The first coach was John Lightfoot and players were from Arlecdon and surrounding villages. Training was on Tuesdays and Thursdays and matches were on Saturday mornings.

From very tentative beginnings, the club grew and eventually got its own change-rooms on the Fairfield, with state of the art bathing facilities, now adjoining the Adams Hall. In 1978, David Farrell became the coach and the club went from strength to strength and at one point fielded three different-age teams. Behind the scenes, Margaret Burns worked tirelessly as Secretary, ably assisted by the committee. Over the years, committee members have come and gone – they were usually parents doing their stint, whilst supporting their children going through the ranks, all with the club's best interest at heart.

Arlecdon's Rugby Playing Youngsters 1980s

Many of the players have gone onto greater things. Stephen Holgate and Craig McDowell have played in the Superleague, whilst Stewart Rickerby, Anthony Huddart, Malcolm Christie, Adam Coulson and Craig Armstrong have played professionally for our local teams. Many, over the years, were selected to play for the County and lots more took their rugby skills up to Open-Age Level.

The club brought a lot of community spirit to the village. Many fund-raising activities have been organised, which were always well supported. These took the form of Bingo, Fun Days, Sponsored Walks, Discos, and Race Nights. Contributions made by the players (both male and female) have never been ignored. Every year there has been a well-organised Presentation Night, often with some Rugby Celebrity there to make a speech and give out trophies and medals. The children have also played in front of very big crowds at Bradford & Wigan. In the summer, there were trips to Morecambe, Blackpool, Whitley Bay, and one year a trip to Wembley. There was always a Xmas Party/Disco with a visit from Father Christmas for the younger ones.

Muriel Gilpin is the longest serving member of the committee (1980 to date) and apart from her dedication to Rugby League in general and the Club in particular, she is no mean soup-maker! Arlecdon's soup had a reputation far and wide – away teams didn't mind getting beat, as they knew they would get some good soup afterwards. Her sister Helen also has long links with the club, as do coaches David Farrell, Stan McCarron and David McDowell, some of them having stood down to make way for a new generation, namely Graeme Gilpin, Mark Shaw and Mark Maudling.

Arlecdon Junior Rugby Club is now over 30 years old and hopefully, it will still be going in another 30 years time. Ron Morgan, ex-Rugby Player, Ehenside Sports Teacher and Rugby commentator, once referred quite rightly, to Arlecdon as 'the little club with a big heart'.

Some more sporting memories of the past...

ARLECDON SCHOOL FOOTBALL TEAM.
COUNTY MOSS SHIELD WINNERS 1940-41

Back L to R, Mr. Walker, C. Pape, C. Grayson, B. Wilson, R. Wright, Mr. Lyle.
Middle L to R, H. Hetherington, J. Vickers, J. Winter, G. Towers, W. Blackburn.
Front L to R, W. Irving & M. Teare

Arlecdon Shool Team 1941-42. Arlecdon Red Rose Hospital Cup Winners 1947

Arlecdon Red Rose Hospital Cup Winners 1947

Above: Arlecdon School Netball Team 1920s. Mr Kirkby, the headmaster is seated at the front with Miss Sweeten (teacher) standing behind him. Nellie Troughton, Annie Lightfoot, Mona Teasdale, Belle Relph and Ella Lavery are among the team members. Don't they look like debutantes?

Left: More lady footballers!

The Queen's Silver Jubilee

Events were organised to celebrate the Queen's Silver Jubilee, twenty five years on the throne.

The nation was celebrating and Arlecdon was to join in and have 'Street Parties'. Noreen Dockray was organising the Parks Road party and the event was to take place down the lonnin' at what was Tile Kiln Farm. There were races for the children and adults alike. 'Miss Lovely Legs', 'Mr Knobbly Knees' and a 'Mr and Mrs' competitions were organised. The children paraded in fancy dress and a good time was had by all.

In the evening a dance was held in Arlecdon Parks farm barn to round off a lovely day.

Top right: Billy Stainton and Fred Shaw in the knobbly knees competition

Right: Brenda and Fred Shaw win second prize in the 'Mr and Mrs' competition

Below: Part of the fancy dress parade

My Memories of Arlecdon Mother and Toddler Club

JEAN BIRDSALL

An off-shoot of Frizington Mother & Toddler Club, Arlecdon Mother & Toddler Club was formed in the early 1980s and led by myself, with the support of a committee. This was at a time when there was quite a large Under-3 population, as the building of Murton Park had attracted many young families to the area.

We met in the Sunday School, although it wasn't the most salubrious of places. I can remember once, when getting the toys out ready for a session, a rat jumped out of the box of dressing-up clothes. Needless to say, the session didn't go ahead and we had to get rid of the dressing-up clothes, as well as wash all the other toys. From that point we transferred our club to the Adams Hall.

When my youngest child started Nursery, I stepped aside and others took over. Over the years since then, there has been mixed fortunes, mainly fluctuating with the birth rate. As I understand it, the club eventually folded, as there weren't enough young children to sustain it.

Looking back, I enjoyed my years at the Club, and I hope that mothers felt it gave their children a good preparation for Nursery School. It's quite a thought that lots of the toddlers who attended then, are now parents with their own babies and toddlers!!

Write Something Every Day

T Irving James – Author and Poet

There are many unmarked graves in St Michael's churchyard but somewhere in this quiet place lie members of the James and Irving families. One William Henry James came from Devon in the mid 19th century probably to work in the mining industry while Joseph Irving was groom and gardener to Captain Burdett of Hakodadi. These two families came together through the marriage of Henry James, a miner and Fanny Irving and produced a talented author and poet, Thomas Irving James.

Irving was the eldest son of Henry and Fanny. He was born in Arlecdon on 13th March 1914 and it soon became apparent that he had paralysis of both legs and his left arm. He spent many months in a Liverpool hospital where he developed pneumonia and was not expected to survive. However, he showed a resilience which was to serve him all his life and survived, only to suffer the terrible blow of his father's death in 1920 from the after effects of a mining accident. Henry James was only 27 years old at the time and as the accident had never been properly reported his wife, Fanny, received no support to bring up her three young children, Irving, Henry and Ilma.

An aunt, who lived on the Isle of Man, wrote to Irving's mother to tell her about a German doctor, a former Harley Street specialist, who was interned there. He was occasionally allowed out of the camp to treat local people. Mrs James took Irving to see him and for 11 weeks he gave Irving specialist massage, under the watchful eye of a camp guard. He asked for no payment, only a photograph of his young patient, explaining that he was only too happy to be able to help those who were sick.

Irving showed significant improvement and was able to walk a little although he mostly crawled about on his hands and knees. When he was old enough to attend Arlecdon School, his mother carried him there and back for many years until, at about the age of nine, Irving had surgery at the famous Oswestry Orthopaedic Hospital and was fitted with leg irons which improved his mobility.

Irving began his writing at school where he was taught by the then headmaster, Mr John Kirby. One of his first poems 'The Christ Child' was set to music and sung as a carol by the church choir. Other poems appeared in the West Cumberland Times and the Whitehaven News in the sections written by 'Denton'.

Mr Kirby continued to encourage Irving throughout his school life and beyond. On one occasion after Irving had shown him a file containing all of his poems, Mr Kirby asked him to compare his work with that of Shakespeare, Milton, Wordsworth and Gray and to burn the lot if it didn't reach anywhere near that standard. Irving duly burnt all his early poems except two, 'Poem Pastoral' and 'To a Bird of Captivity', both of which appeared much later in his first book of poems, 'Stammerings'.

Irving despaired of ever finding work after he left school in common with many of his former classmates. It was the 1930s, a time of great unemployment in the area. The picture of unemployed men shuffling on street corners with no chance of work must have remained in Irving's mind and led to his writing the following poem:

Unemployed

Will they stand in groups again,
Shabby, hungry, broken men
coughing, cursing, pacing.....pacing,
smoking, talking football, racing,
hands thrust deep in trouser pockets,
fingering their pitmen's dockets,
wishing it had been a shilling,
killing time, while time is killing –
killing body, killing soul,
dying slowly on the dole?

For I have seen
pit mounds grow green,
and pithead gear
rust year by year,
gloom settle down
upon the town,
and, like a fog,
it's breathing clog,
until, until
it's pulse stood still.

And I have heard
the whispered word
that so-and-so
was soon to go,
heard too, the vans
with pots and pans
at dawn of day
speed on their way,
to Leicester, London?
God knows where! Gone!

And I recall uncurtained windows, where
children read aloud a notice there:
HOUSE TO LET, as weeks went by,
ceased to fascinate the eye;
one by one, the panes were cracked,
JACK LOVES JUNE in woodwork hacked;
slates dislodged made rafters rotten,
the crumbling walls cried out "forgotten"
echoing the bitter mood
of people with less hope than food.

However, after more surgery, his mobility improved but further changes were to take place in Irving's life. His mother had remarried and his stepfather was offered a job in Wolverhampton through the influences of the Rev. A.J. Wilson, a former vicar of Arlecdon.

The family moved from a quiet country area to a busy industrial town which must have had a depressing effect on Irving and caused him to begin another poem thus:

> '*Some day I shall arise and leave this town behind*
> *With all its evil smells, its jostling crowds begrimed.*'

For a while things appeared to go from bad to worse. Recovery from even more surgery was almost complete when he slipped, while sitting near the fire, and upset a pan full of boiling water over himself. This resulted in severe scalding of his back and right arm and meant that he had to spend another seven months immobilised in bed. A lesser person might have given up but it would appear that Irving used this imposed inactivity to formulate his ideas and poems, one of which explains that he was forced to 'stand aloof' and take the role of 'curbside (sic) critic' and ends:

> '*Why seek ye then with pity to intrude*
> *On this my elevated solitude?*'

Irving's fortunes began to improve when he met Robert Moss, a writer, who undertook to train him in journalism. He began to contribute articles to local newspapers and might have continued this occupation but for the Second World War which meant that he was able to obtain work in the inspection department of a Midlands arms factory.

After the war he continued to work as an inspector in the Machine Products Department of Marston Fordhouses, later a subsidiary of ICI, where his winning entry in a short story competition resulted in him writing it up into a full length novel, a mystery thriller, 'Death

Ilma, Peter, Irving and Grandma James

Henry James

Irving James

after Dinner'. He desperately needed someone to type up the work and a friend introduced him to a Miss Edna Rigby, the lady who later became his wife. Edna prepared and typed all his manuscripts for a further two thrillers and his collections of poetry.

This courageous man's advice to aspiring writers was:

'Write something, however short, every day. Keep at it and don't give up, even if you have enough rejection slips to paper Buckingham Palace as I did. If you want to find plots, they're everywhere – in the papers, in odd scraps of conversation, in people's lives. If you're a writer you'll never be stuck for a story.'

What encouraging advice from a man who overcame such adversity. Perhaps he inherited this stamina and determination from his mother – this young woman, left widowed with three children, who thought nothing of carrying her son to and from school, spent many anxious hours at his hospital bedside, nursed him through countless illnesses and still found the energy to support him in his writing during those long periods of recuperation. Fanny Irving is as deserving of our admiration as her talented son.

Thomas Irving James died in 1984 aged 70 years.

With grateful thanks for information provided by Irving's nephew, Peter and his wife Valerie.

History Group members, Pat Smith and Jean Birdsall chat to Peter and Valerie James. Peter is the nephew of Irving James

Arlecdon Sunday School

RECOLLECTIONS FROM JEAN BIRDSALL

Built in 1878, the same year as the school, the Sunday School building has played host to a variety of different functions over the years.

Obviously in the late 1800s and early 1900s, when Arlecdon was thriving, attendance at the Sunday School was very good.

My recollections of the Sunday School are from the 1950s onwards, and before the Adams Hall was built, it was the focal point of the village, with such events as church meetings, harvest sales and suppers, Mothers' Union, church and village fund-raising functions, local wedding receptions and probably a children's Sunday School, but I wasn't aware of one.

Arlecdon Sunday School

In the early 1980s, the Sunday School was resurrected by the Rev. Nicholas Dixon, with myself as the teacher, ably assisted by Ruth Wilson, a local lass and pupil at Ehenside. We met every Sunday morning, and with fairly small numbers, we were able to do quite a lot of practical things such as art and craft, acting out playlets, singing, bible stories and learning relevant prayers, making the subject of Religion more interesting. On special occasions, e.g. Christmas, Easter, Harvest, Mothers' Day, we went into church and performed – congregation's numbers were always up on those days as proud parents came to watch their children.

As children grew older and moved on, or interest waned after a few years, the Sunday Club, as it was called, was disbanded. After that, it was held in the church during the morning service. Probably the 80s saw the building used the most. Arlecdon Junior Rugby Club used it for a while as change-rooms; there was a Mother and Toddler Club, a Youth Club, Bingo and other fund-raising, Holiday Playschemes, as well as church events. The building needed quite a lot spent on it and went into decline. Round about 1990, it was bought and converted into a rather attractive dwelling, so signalling the end of the Sunday School for community use in Arlecdon.

Will Watson

William Watson was born in Aspatria in 1887; his father was a manager of Wardhall quarry. When Wardhall quarry closed they moved to Rowrah Hall.

Will attended Arlecdon school where he formed a classroom friendship with Jack Adams who later became Lord Adams of Ennerdale.

In 1910 Will went to Canada at the age of 23 to work for the Canadian Pacific Railways, at Moose Jaw Saskatchewan, later moving to Vancouver in British Columbia, where he became Secretary of Vancouver Island Branch of United Mineworkers.

On his return to England after six years absence he married Sarah Johnson known as Sally, from Springwell House Bullgill in 1917. Among the guests were the future Lord and Lady Adams. He and Jack remained friends and colleagues in several walks of life each being chairman in turn of the old Arlecdon and Frizington Urban Council, later to become Ennerdale Rural District Council and, later still, Copeland Council.

Will and Sally lived at 28 Parks Road. Will went on to become the third generation of quarry managers, supervising operations at Kelton Head, Salter Hall, Egremont Clints, Rowrah Head and Rowrah Hall, all of which provided the limestone for the United Steel Works blast furnaces.

He was also the manager of his old school at Arlecdon and later became a member of the Southern Area Education Committee and a governor of Whitehaven Grammar School.

He retired in 1958 and lived for a short time at Maryport before moving to Cockermouth.

In 1977 Will and Sally celebrated their Diamond Wedding (60 years of marriage) at the age of 90 years. They both died in their 100th year in 1987, just missing their 70 years of marriage and their 100th birthdays.

*Dumper truck driver
– Joe Bill Relph*

Quarry workers – Brian Wilkinson, Terence McVeigh Taylor, and Percy Richardson

The marriage of William Watson and Sarah

Rowrah Methodist Chapel

In his leaflet 'Rowrah Old Chapel 1839-96', Mr J.C. Dent describes how Methodism came to Rowrah in 1839, when the 'Centenary Chapel' was built, one hundred years after the conversion of John Wesley. It stood on the roadside at Chapel Row, which was the original main road to Cockermouth via Middle Leys, before the present road was built in the 1930s.

It would appear that William Sibson and Joseph Yates of Rowrah Hall and other neighbouring farmers were responsible for raising the money for the building, which could accommodate 200 people.

Mr Dent describes an article in the 'Weslyan Methodist Recorder' of 1896 written by the Rev. W. H. Mosley, which tells of the visit of a Whitehaven minister, the Rev. W. Morley Punshon, to Rowrah Chapel in 1846.

The Rev. Punshon portrayed the route from Whitehaven as 'lonely, wild land, patched with field and heather'. He reported that after following the road over Hensingham Hill and Richmond Hill there were only a few isolated houses (no terraced houses at Frizington or Arlecdon) and an old inn. He named Tile Kiln Cottages, Arlecdon Parks, Rowrah Head and Rowrah Hall.

Rowrah Chapel
by Reg Goodman

ROWRAH
METHODIST CHURCH

Despite these scattered communities, the chapel was nearly full when he arrived. He noted that there were some present who had walked from Cockermouth, a distance of ten miles and a pitman, Robert Seeds had walked from Greysouthen and would reach home in the early morning, just in time to change into his pit clothes and go to work!

Other interesting members of the congregation included Jacob Fletcher, a Beckermet farmer, described by the Rev. Punshon as 'tall, thin, and sallow, with a high pitched voice and an

Rowrah Chapel circa 1940

almost irresistible power from God'. Another, John Rigg ' a mole catcher, short, square built, brown haired, moving from farm to farm, taking heaven with him, saving all he can so that he may buy stockings for poor labourer's children and leave behind him a sum between £10 and £30 for all the chapels in debt, on condition that they shake themselves free.'

He goes on to name John Douglas, a penniless lad, taken from the workhouse by a Methodist dyer and taught the trade, who became 'a mighty preacher'. But perhaps the most remarkable character was William Irving, a beautiful singer of gigantic size and great physical strength. Since his conversion at a revival meeting at Dearham, he had given up deeds of wanton violence and acquired the habit of Christian self control. He worked as a steward on an estate near Rowrah and he was once shot at by a local mason when he was carrying £200 to pay the estate iron workers. In spite of his wounds he ran after his assailant, but only disarmed him 'forbearing to punish him within an inch of his life'.

Rowrah Chapel today

The 'Old Chapel' was replaced in 1896 by a new building large enough to accommodate the increasing population of miners and quarry workers who inhabited the terraced houses on Arlecdon Hill and Rowrah Road. The architect for the new chapel was Mr Arthur Huddart. The builder was Mr Green of Pardshaw and the total cost was under £1000.

There were over 400 people at the dedication service which was conducted by the Rev. H. J. Pope of Manchester who also took the evening service, where he again preached to an even larger congregation, some of whom could not get into the chapel!

Arlecdon Brownies, one of the groups who used the chapel rooms

The chapel building became a focal point for many village activities. There was a large Sunday School with anniversaries and trips, via the railway, to Seascale.

The chapel choir performed cantatas and services of song at other churches in the Circuit. They also performed operettas under various choir leaders including, Albert Bethwaite, William Gilmore and Hannah Thompson. There was an active Wesley Guild and Mrs Rothery, who was the organist at one time, started a Girls' Friendly Society which was greatly enjoyed. The Brownies met in the Sunday School rooms in the 1990s. At one time, the whole of local village life revolved around the chapel.

Sadly, by the end of the 20th century, the congregation had declined and the decision was taken to close the chapel in 1996 – its centenary year. The chapel was sold and is now converted into two private dwellings.

Information obtained from leaflets 'Rowrah Old Chapel' by Mr J. C. Dent and 'Centenary of Rowrah Methodist Church' by Mr L. Davies.

St Michael's Church Arlecdon Bellringing Team 2005

Prior to the restoration of the church in 1903 Arlecdon had two bells chimed using ropes attached by levers, one of the original bells is kept in the Ringing Room. The Tower was built and the 8 bells installed during the period of 1903 -1905. The current bells have ropes attached via wheels thus allowing more control and the ability to ring changes.

The 1903 – 1905 bells were given by the following people:-

1st.	Rev. Richard Taylor, a former vicar
2nd.	Messers J. R. and J. Watson of South Mosses
3rd	Mrs Eleanor Jackson and family of The Result Frizington, formerly of Bigcroft
4th.	The family of Mrs Spedding, Main Street Frizington
5th.	The parishioners generally
6th.	Mr J. F. Mossop and Mr W Fletcher
7th.	Mr J. F. Mossop and Mr W Fletcher
8th.	Mr Joseph Gouldie of The Gill, Bromfield, a former resident of the parish

Since then many local people have learned to ring the St Michael's church bells. The current members of St Michael's bell ringing team are people who have been born locally and others who have moved into the area. Arlecdon has a reputation for being a good place to learn, perhaps due to its rural location.

Practice night is Thursday between 7.30pm and 9pm. Regular service ringing is 10.30am to 11am on the second and fourth Sundays of the month. Ringing is also often required for Weddings, Funerals and other local and national events. Bell ringing has been a way of communicating events of national, spiritual and religious significance to local people for centuries, for example it was the general tradition to ring a different number of times for the death of a man, woman or a child in the parish, or as a warning for fire or war.

Back Row L to R: Mark Cubey, Deryk Rostron, John Wilkinson (Tower Captain). Front Row L to R: Rita Lee, Hayley Barton, Marilyn Rostron, Lucy Richards, Rosanne Wilkinson Missing Edwin Matthews

There is an ongoing need for local people to learn to ring the bells for another century. It is a good way to meet people and contribute to the local community.

Learning to ring is never ending; an enjoyable challenge and you don't have to be musical, clever or strong. For young people, bell ringing is an activity that can contribute to 'The Duke of Edinburgh Award' scheme; there is no upper age limit for learning to ring.

In June 2007 St. Michael's Church hosted the Annual Striking Competition organised by the Carlisle Guild of Church Bellringers in which seven bands of ringers took part. St. Michael's, Arlecdon won the competition. This was the latest of several successes in recent years by a team made up from St. Michael's ringers and regular visitors from other local towers.

The Stork Hotel at Rowrah

The first tenant of the Stork Hotel, Rowrah, was Jane Holliday, a widow with five children.

A Mr Dalzell from Harrington Brewery asked her if she would be interested in taking over the tenancy of a new public house in Rowrah in 1865. Rowrah had a fast growing community due to the influx of workers in the iron-ore industry and the development of the railway system.

Three of Jane's children were in farm service but her youngest son, David, and daughter, Bella, moved to Rowrah with their mother. Bella later took over the tenancy from her mother and continued as landlady for 59 years.

David eventually set up a carrier service and from his meticulous record keeping it is possible to see the mode of transport and the journeys made by former inhabitants towards the end of the nineteenth century.

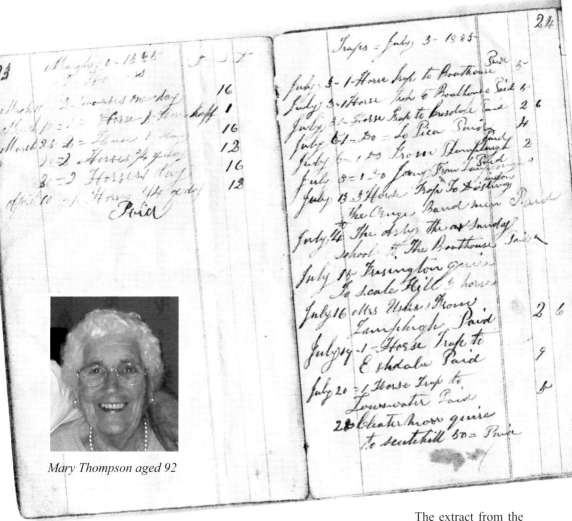

Mary Thompson aged 92

The extract from the account book was kindly loaned by Mary Thompson, David's granddaughter, who lives on Pasture Road, Rowrah. Mary recalls the story of the time a member of the Royal Family came to open the YMCA in the early 1900s. Some comfortable chairs were needed and so they were borrowed from Mary's grandmother, Mrs Jobson, at the Stork Hotel but she was not invited to the ceremony – and was she mad!! She refused to go and watch the event saying, "Ah wadn't gaa foot!" meaning she wouldn't step over the threshold. It's a wonder she didn't go and take her chairs back before the proceedings got underway.

Mary also remembers how many Arlecdon and Rowrah families emigrated to find work during the depression of the 1920s. Her father went to British Columbia, Canada to work in the coalfields. Her mother followed months later with Mary and her siblings. They travelled across Canada by train for over a week to reach him.

Unfortunately her father had an accident in the mine and was unable to continue working and so they had to return home.

The late Gladys Gainford recalls in the Rowrah Chapel Centenary leaflet written by Les Davies in 1996:

"I remember the tears as we sang 'God be with you 'till we meet again.' as people left to go abroad, waving them off at Rowrah Station. They were pioneers who suffered hard times and home-sickness. I have visited families in Vancouver who talked of a week on the train across Canada, with young children, as they travelled to join their men who had gone ahead, building their own houses, sinking their own wells and so on. Their families have come here on holiday and told of the privations they suffered: but of course they have reaped the rewards."

Rowrah Station and Signal Box. Photo courtesy Cumbrian Railways Association

The Stork Hotel today. Proprieters Paul and Joan Kerswell (Note the gentlemen's urinal in the foreground – a listed building perhaps?)

The Adams Hall

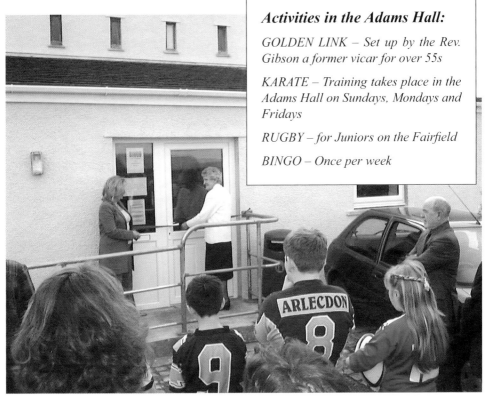

Activities in the Adams Hall:

GOLDEN LINK – Set up by the Rev. Gibson a former vicar for over 55s

KARATE – Training takes place in the Adams Hall on Sundays, Mondays and Fridays

RUGBY – for Juniors on the Fairfield

BINGO – Once per week

Mary Lightfoot opens the newly refurbished Adams Hall in 2004

Arlecdon Schoolchildren entertain the members of Lunch Club which meets on the first Tuesday in each month

Changes, changes...

Public Transport is very infrequent. Buses pass through the village on their journey from Cockermouth to Cleator Moor.

Some earlier forms of transport

Isaac Jackson of Hakodadi circa 1916

Ready for an outing - Henry Edmund Jackson and his sisters are on the front row

Nan Parker as 'Britannia' travels in style 1953   *NOT recommended!!*

Schools

Ehenside School closed this year which means that secondary education for Arlecdon and Frizington children will now be provided at the West Lakes Academy at Egremont

Quite different to the days long ago when children would complete their education in the village school unless they won a scholarship to go to the Grammar School at Whitehaven.

Arlecdon had a good record of passes over the years.

In 1929, one lad, Ernest Smith, won 'The Florence Exhibition' (£50 per annum during school life) – a lot of money in those days. This enabled him to take up his place at Whitehaven Grammar School. Ernest was one of a family of six who lived at Winder Brow.

The 'Florence Exhibition' was a competition founded by Mr G. Dickinson of Red How, Lamplugh in memory of his late wife.

Arlecdon School 1920s. Ernest Smith is the second child from the right on the back row

Mary Williamson — mother of Don Hunter.
3rd child from left. Second row.

Housing

Phyllis Tomlinson's notebook records that new council houses were let at Arlecdon in 1957 followed by new bungalows in 1966. Murton Park Estate was built in the 1970/80s.

Quite a change from the rows of terraced houses built for the miners and quarry workers a century earlier.

One of these builders was a Joseph McQuire who built Long Row, formerly named McQuire's Row.

Standing, Mary Taylor, Martha Snook, William (McQuire) Martin, Martin Taylor. Seated – Joseph McQuire holding John McQuire, Martha McQuire and Elizabeth (Boadle) McQuire holding Margaret McQuire – circa 1890

Other Local News

A new Water Treatment Plant was installed on the Low Road by United Utilities - 2006

Wind farms – Planning permission has been give to erect a wind farm on Moresby Moor

Re-refurbishment of Church tower – The church tower has been repaired and made watertight thanks to a substantial grant from the Aggregates Fund.

The new Rector, the Reverend Jacqueline Curtis and Vicar, the Reverend Peter Turnbull were licensed on Monday 14th July 2008

Arlecdon History Group

Typing up research

Collecting information

Sorting out the material for the book

Photo by Simon Ledingham

Above: St Michael's church and churchyard and below recording memorial inscriptions

Recording memorial inscriptions in St Michael's churchyard

Right: Feeding the workers

Below: Exhibition 2005

Interviewees Nan Wilson and Mary Thompson exchange amusing stories

Lunch Club members visit Frizington CDC to help

Jean Birdsall getting ready to record

*Maureen Fisher with Tom Tyson
at 'The Music Farm' recording
voiceovers for the DVD*